POSITIVELY
ENERGIZING
LEADERSHIP

Other Books by Kim Cameron

Coffin Nails and Corporate Strategies (1982), with Robert H. Miles

Organizational Effectiveness: A Comparison of Multiple Models (1983), with David A. Whetten

Paradox and Transformation: Toward a Theory of Change in Organization and Management (1988), with Robert E. Quinn

Organizational Decline: Conceptual, Empirical, and Normative Foundations (1988), with Robert I. Sutton and David A. Whetten

Positive Organizational Scholarship: Foundations of a New Discipline (2003), with Jane E. Dutton and Robert E. Quinn

Leading with Values: Positivity, Virtues, and High Performance (2006), with Edward D. Hess

Competing Values Leadership: Creating Value in Organizations (2006) with Robert E. Quinn, Jeff DeGraff, and Anjan V. Thakor

Making the Impossible Possible: Leading Extraordinary Performance—The Rocky Flats Story (2006), with Marc Lavine

The Virtuous Organization: Insights from Some of the World's Leading Management Thinkers (2008), with Charles C. Manz, Karen P. Manz, and Robert D. Marx

Organizational Effectiveness (2010)

Diagnosing and Changing Organizational Culture: Based on the Competing Values Framework (3rd Edition) (2011), with Robert E. Quinn

The Oxford Handbook of Positive Organizational Scholarship (2012) with Gretchen M. Spreitzer

Positive Leadership: Strategies for Extraordinary Performance (2nd Edition) (2012)

Practicing Positive Leadership: Tools and Techniques That Create Extraordinary Results (2013)

Developing Management Skills (10th Edition) (2020), with David A. Whetten

POSITIVELY ENERGIZING LEADERSHIP

VIRTUOUS ACTIONS AND RELATIONSHIPS THAT CREATE HIGH PERFORMANCE

KIM CAMERON

BK
Berrett–Koehler Publishers, Inc.

Berrett-Koehler Publishers, Inc.
1333 Broadway, Suite 1000
Oakland, CA 94612-1921
Tel: (510) 817-2277   Fax: (510) 817-2278   www.bkconnection.com

Ordering Information

Quantity sales. Special discounts are available on quantity purchases by corporations, associations, and others. For details, contact the "Special Sales Department" at the Berrett-Koehler address above.

Individual sales. Berrett-Koehler publications are available through most bookstores. They can also be ordered directly from Berrett-Koehler: Tel: (800) 929-2929; Fax: (802) 864-7626; www.bkconnection.com.

Orders for college textbook / course adoption use. Please contact Berrett-Koehler: Tel: (800) 929-2929; Fax: (802) 864-7626.

Distributed to the U.S. trade and internationally by Penguin Random House Publisher Services.

Berrett-Koehler and the BK logo are registered trademarks of Berrett-Koehler Publishers, Inc.

Printed in the United States of America

Berrett-Koehler books are printed on long-lasting acid-free paper. When it is available, we choose paper that has been manufactured by environmentally responsible processes. These may include using trees grown in sustainable forests, incorporating recycled paper, minimizing chlorine in bleaching, or recycling the energy produced at the paper mill.

Library of Congress Cataloging-in-Publication Data

Names: Cameron, Kim S., author.
Title: Positively energizing leadership : virtuous actions and relationships that create high performance / Kim Cameron.
Description: Oakland, CA : Berrett-Koehler Publishers, [2021] | Includes bibliographical references and index.
Identifiers: LCCN 2021013080 | ISBN 9781523093830 (paperback) | ISBN 9781523093847 (adobe pdf) | ISBN 9781523093854 (epub)
Subjects: LCSH: Leadership. | Organizational effectiveness—Management. | Interpersonal relations.
Classification: LCC HD57.7 .C3539 2021 | DDC 658.4/092—dc23
LC record available at https://lccn.loc.gov/2021013080

First Edition

27 26 25 24 23 22 21   10 9 8 7 6 5 4 3 2 1

Book producer: Westchester Publishing Services
Cover designer: Howie Severson

CONTENTS

 PREFACE

This book is about one of the most important factors in accounting for spectacular performance in organizations and their employees: the positive energy displayed by leaders. The book relies on validated scientific evidence to make the case that all individuals are inherently attracted to and flourish in the presence of positive energy. Most importantly, the book provides evidence that leaders' virtuous behaviors are tightly linked to their positive energy and to extraordinarily positive performance in their organizations. Virtuous practices on the part of leaders are key in accounting for the highest levels of positive performance.

Practical suggestions are provided in the book for how to assess positive energy, how to develop it, and how to help leaders implement it in order to elevate their organizations' performance. The prescriptions offered in the book are also relevant in families, in relationships, in community service, and in classrooms. Thus, not only is positively energizing leadership a major predictor of success in private and public sector organizations, but it is applicable in more personal settings as well. Students who have been exposed to positively energizing leadership, for example, perform significantly better on academic tests as well as experience higher levels of well-being than students not so exposed.

This book is intended to be helpful to leaders in almost any kind of organization, to individuals facing trying times or experiencing difficult challenges, to educators attempting to help their students flourish personally and academically, and to those interested in enhancing their relationships with family and friends. Providing helpful prescriptions as well as the empirical evidence that validates them is an important purpose of this book.

Many individuals have had an important impact on the work cited in this book. I have especially benefited from the expertise of the publications staff at Berrett-Koehler and my friends and editors Steve Piersanti and Jeevan Sivasubramaniam. My colleagues Jane Dutton and Bob Quinn have taught me a great deal and have provided unmeasurable emotional and intellectual support in addition to collaborating in founding the Center for Positive Organizations. Colleague Wayne Baker introduced me to the concept of positive energy, which started me on a research path that helped spawn this book, and colleague Brad Owens played a major role in initiating this research stream. The staff at the Center for Positive Organizations at the University of Michigan—Angie Ceely, Betsy Erwin, Hitomi Katsumi, Esther Kyte, Sue Reuhle, Stacey Scimeca, and Katie Trevathan—have set a standard of extraordinary performance that truly exemplifies positively energizing leadership. Most importantly, my wife, Melinda, has been the most positively energizing leader I have ever known and has exemplified virtuous practices every single day for more than 50 years.

INTRODUCTION
Leading through Positive Relational Energy

Recent events including earthquakes, floods, tornadoes, cyberattacks, ethical lapses, wildfires, and the worldwide COVID-19 pandemic have created a confluence of challenges that most of us have not experienced in our lifetimes. Racial injustice, economic devastation, and loss of life have elevated our collective consciousness regarding what is wrong in our world. Contention, outrage, and violence have become widespread. Extensive economic, emotional, and health effects have changed normal daily activities, relationships, institutions, and even values.

One response to these conditions has been an increased emphasis on how to stay positive, how to find happiness, and how to enhance well-being in trying times. In fact, tens of thousands of books are listed on Amazon on positivity, on happiness, and on well-being. Likewise, social media is filled with advice on how to cope with anxiety, stress, depression, and apprehension through the use of special diets and menus, physical fitness training, meditation, and positive thinking. Positivity has turned into a bit of a fad, and entries appearing in the media have escalated in the face of negative events.

The trouble is, when people are struggling emotionally, stressed from the loss of loved ones, jobs, or relationships, or just gritting through difficult days, it is often hard to be positive.[1] "Happiology"[2] is not exactly a preferred prescription for coping with tragedy. Not only that, but leaders in organizations often balk at interventions that focus on positivity, asserting that the daily pressures of managing bottom-line performance in turbulent times consume their time and attention. Positive practices are simply a deflection from real-world pressures, they say. Positivity is merely a feel-good side trip.

The National Labor Relations Board, in fact, recently issued a ruling against T-Mobile's provision requiring that workers "maintain a positive work environment," recognizing that directing employees to be positive may do more harm than good, ironically generating cynicism, resistance, burnout, and even outright hostility.[3] Mandated positivity can come across as uncompassionate toward those who are mourning the deaths of friends and relatives, the loss of jobs, and disrupted in-person connections. They may not even feel capable of positivity. This problem highlights one of the major differences between this book and a multiplicity of "positivity" books on the market.

This book is not about positivity, happiology, or unbridled optimism. It is about how to capitalize on an inherent tendency in all living systems to orient themselves toward light or life-giving positive energy. It relies firmly on empirical evidence to describe the extraordinary results of positive energy in the workplace.

The basic message is this: all human beings flourish in the presence of light or of positive energy. This tendency is known as the heliotropic effect, a concept adapted from a phenomenon typically ascribed to how plants respond to the sun's rays. The heliotropic effect is a scientifically verified phenomenon that has not yet been applied in the social and organizational sciences.

Chapter 1 provides empirical evidence that the heliotropic effect influences individuals and that it provides an important way to cope with difficulties as well as with abundance. The evidence verifies that all human beings respond favorably to and are renewed by positive energy, and this book shows how to implement the heliotropic principle in practical ways.

The kind of positive energy that most accounts for flourishing in individuals and in organizations is called *relational energy*. This book explains how relational energy is created and enhanced through the demonstration of virtuous actions (e.g., generosity, compassion, gratitude, trustworthiness, forgiveness, and kindness). Virtuousness, especially as demonstrated by leaders, produces extraordinarily positive outcomes in individuals and their organizations, particularly in trying times and in situations of loss or grief. The empirical evidence confirming these outcomes is reviewed in chapters 2, 3, and 4.

Mandating that employees behave positively, think happy thoughts, or be cheerful when they are depressed, anxious, or experiencing emotional pain produces false positivity. It is inauthentic, disingenuous, dishonest, and untrustworthy. It denies reality, which is the opposite of virtuous responses in trying times. The reason virtuousness is so crucial in these conditions is precisely because it helps people cope in a genuine and authentic way. Positive relational energy increases rather than decreases when virtuousness is displayed.

For example, studies show that individuals who suffered the loss of loved ones but who subsequently became stronger as a result, learned to appreciate life more, and flourished personally had experienced others' virtuous actions—compassion, authenticity, kindness, and higher purpose.[4]

Empirical evidence suggests that organizations as well as individuals achieve significant improvement in trying times when leaders are the role models of virtuous behavior. In one large financial services organization, for example, the CEO, John Kim, credited positively energizing leadership for the dramatic success achieved by his organization:

> Implementing positively energizing leadership was initially seen as just being positive—smiles. It became clear, however, that this was a significant change. . . . There is no end, no final grade. This is about changing our culture, our strategy, and our approach. It is not a destination or a conclusion but a process. I will know that we have succeeded when customers and employees see us as above average in all the technical aspects of our business, but then by succeeding above all

FIGURE 1.1

Virtuousness, positive relational energy, and performance

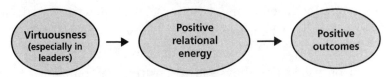

understanding. We don't debate how we will get there. We just take initiative. If I wanted to stop this movement I couldn't. It's way beyond my control. People are doing things now that are self-perpetuating.[5]

John's success included achieving profitability growth at four times the industry average, dramatic increases in employee well-being, significant decreases in employee turnover, and customer loyalty rates among the best in the industry.[6]

This book establishes the fact that an inclination toward virtuousness develops naturally in early infancy,[7] that virtuousness produces positive relational energy, and that virtuousness in leaders is associated with positive outcomes in organizations. Figure 1.1 summarizes this central argument.

POSITIVE ENERGY IN LEADERS

A great deal of research confirms that leaders are vital in affecting the performance of organizations and their employees. In fact, between 20 and 70 percent of the variance in organizations' performance is attributable to leadership behavior.[8] No other factor—culture, strategy, processes, incentive systems—is as important.[9] There-fore, this book highlights key attributes of positively energizing leaders and describes some practices and activities that help foster these positive outcomes. Virtuous behaviors demonstrated by leaders are important not only because they lead to positive outcomes (e.g., profitability, productivity, employee engagement) but also because they lead to the only kind of energy that does not deplete with use and does not require recovery time after it is expended. Whereas physical, emotional, and mental energy diminish with use, relational energy elevates. Virtuousness lies at the heart of positively energizing leadership and relational energy.

It is important to point out that positively energizing leaders are not self-aggrandizing, dominant individuals who seek the limelight. They are not always in charge or at the front. They are not necessarily extroverts and assertive in their demeanor. They are, rather, individuals who produce growth, development, and improvement among others with whom they interact. They exude a certain kind of light that is uplifting and helps others become their best. An apropos definition is a variation of a statement by John Quincy Adams from more than 200 years ago:

> If your actions inspire others to dream more, learn more, do more, and become more, you are a positively energizing leader.

One exemplary role model of positively energizing leadership is a friend and colleague, Jim Mallozzi, a former CEO of one of the Prudential Financial Services businesses. Jim's life as a leader has been marked by positive energy, positive leadership, and, as a result, positive results.

Jim was appointed CEO of the Prudential Real Estate and Relocation (PRERS) business when the organization was struggling. Employee morale was in the tank. Some customers were so dissatisfied that PRERS actually paid them a premium to remain as customers. The firm was $70 million in the red when Jim was appointed, and the previous year it had lost $140 million.

It's nice to talk about being positively energizing when things are going well, but in difficult times, when all the indicators are going in the wrong direction, when finger-pointing and blaming are rampant, a positive perspective is usually seen as soft, syrupy, touchy-feely, Pollyannaish, and, frankly, just plain irrelevant. As a quintessential positively energizing leader, Jim said the following upon taking over the CEO role:

> When I took over, we were facing a 70 million dollar loss per year. The company had lost 140 million dollars the year before. I harkened back to my previous experience in the company and what I learned about positively energizing leadership. The message was, let's look at what we have as opposed to what we don't have. Let's look at what we can do as opposed to what we don't do. How do we start to take the limits off our company, not in terms of just going back to where we were two years or five years ago, but how do we achieve something that is truly great and never seen before in our industry? We

implemented a variety of positive practices and tools, and the results were astounding.[10]

The results, in fact, were astonishing. In 12 months PRERS went from a $70 million loss to a $20 million profit. The firm won the J.D. Power Award for Service (the nation's most prestigious), and some customers gave PRERS a 100 percent satisfaction rating. Employee opinion scores increased in 9 of 10 categories. The firm's financial performance doubled what the business plan predicted. Voluntary turnover declined. And, when Warren Buffett's company, Berkshire Hathaway, acquired PRERS a few years later, its stock price was well above the stock price of the parent company.

It's not just in his role as CEO, however, that Jim exemplified positive energizing leadership. It extended to his personal life as well. For example, one day Jim received a phone call from his wife, Maureen, reporting that his daughter's high school grades had just been issued. He was told that he needed to talk with his daughter about a disastrous grade in one of her classes. Her grades looked like this:

ENGLISH:	A
HISTORY:	A
CHEMISTRY:	A
MATH:	D
HUMANITIES:	A

The normal reaction for most parents is to focus on the abysmal grade in math class. It's natural to concentrate primarily on what's gone wrong. On the other hand, Jim didn't abandon his positively energizing approach to problems, even at home, and this is essentially the way he approached the situation.

JIM: I need to talk to you about your report card.
DAUGHTER: Yeah, I know, dad.
JIM: I want to talk to you about your grade in English.
DAUGHTER: But I got an A in English.
JIM: I know you did. But I want to talk about English. Do you like your teacher?
DAUGHTER: I like her a lot.
JIM: Do you get your homework in on time, and do you participate in class?
DAUGHTER: Every day.
JIM: Do you go in after class to ask questions or check on assignments?
DAUGHTER: Yeah. I've gone in several times.
JIM: Do you have a study group to prepare for exams and assignments?
DAUGHTER: Several of us get together to study and help each other out.
JIM: Look, Sweetheart. You are an A student. You know how to get As. But now let's talk about math. Do you like your teacher?
DAUGHTER: I think he is a jerk.
JIM: Do you get your homework in on time, and do you participate in class?
DAUGHTER: Heck no. I don't understand the material.
JIM: Do you go in after class to ask questions or check on assignments?

DAUGHTER: No. I probably should, but I don't want to appear stupid.

JIM: Do you have a study group to prepare for exams and assignments?

DAUGHTER: No, I don't want others to know how bad I am at math.

JIM: Well, Sweetheart, why don't you just apply in math class what you know how to do to get As in English? I will check with you every Friday, and I'll ask you about these things. You don't have to like your teacher, but you have to respect him. I want to encourage you to participate in class each day, even if it is just to raise your hand and ask the teacher to repeat what he just said. In addition, consider going in after class and checking with the teacher about what is confusing. If you don't get it, a lot of others don't either, so why don't you put together a study group to help each other out? And if you don't get your homework done because you don't understand it, let me know, and we'll get you some help. Will you do it?

DAUGHTER: OK, sure, dad.

It's not hard to guess what her grade was in math at the end of the next semester.

This book explains what is meant by positive energy, how it relates to leadership, and what its effects are on the lives of individuals and the organizations in which they are employed. In addition to providing examples and stories, the book also provides validated empirical research to confirm all of the prescriptions.

Evidence is important because when results count, when desired outcomes need to be ensured, when impact is significant, scientific validity is crucial. None of us would subject ourselves to a physician who practiced medicine on the basis of a magazine article, an inspiring story, or an interesting example. We would need to be confident that his or her medical practice is based on credible, validated science. The same is true in organizations. Because leaders have a significant impact on the performance of organizations, it is important that when we give advice to leaders, evidence exists that what we are prescribing is credible and valid. This is why this book is careful to provide the scientific references and the relevant data that validate the prescriptions in this book.

OVERVIEW

Chapter 1 explains what is meant by positive energy and why all human beings have an inherent inclination toward it. The key concept is the heliotropic effect: the natural tendency in all living systems to orient themselves toward light and life-giving positive energy. Chapter 2 explains the importance of positively energizing leadership in organizations and individuals. In chapter 3, the key attributes of positive energizers are enumerated, and the research confirming their impact on organizational performance as well as on employees is summarized. Chapter 4 highlights some behaviors and practices that are seldom linked to positive energy but that are heliotropic and foster positive energy and positive outcomes.

Several examples of organizations that have capitalized on positive energy are discussed in chapter 5 as well as what they did to achieve outstanding performance. The book includes several practical applications that have been utilized in organizations in which I have conducted research. Chapter 6 addresses a variety of objections to a positive perspective and to positive energy as a topic. Some suggestions that address these objections and criticisms are offered so that readers can be confident in the validity and utility of positive energy, positive leadership, and positive practices.

Three supplemental resources are provided: resource 1 identifies several methods for measuring positive energy in leaders, resource 2 identifies some of the practices that foster it, and resource 3 provides discussion questions that may assist in teaching and coaching situations as well as in enhancing application.

1
FORMS OF ENERGY AND THE HELIOTROPIC EFFECT

The rapidly changing and unpredictable environment being experienced by much of the world's population might accurately be described as "VUCA," an acronym coined by the U.S. military that refers to volatile, uncertain, complex, and ambiguous conditions. Varying directions from national leaders and organizations, contradictory scientific findings, and a barrage of social media advice for how to cope with the anxiety, stress, and apprehension have often produced more confusion than clarity. In such circumstances, an important principle becomes ever more relevant: *In order to effectively manage turbulent circumstances, we must identify something that is stable, universal, and constant.*

Consider the case of John Kennedy Jr., the son of the 35th president of the United States. John was flying his private plane from New Jersey to Martha's Vineyard in Massachusetts when the conditions became dark and cloudy. He had been trained to fly by sight navigation but not by instrumentation through conditions of invisibility. He ended up flying the plane into the ocean, killing himself, his wife, and her sister. He had not known he was headed toward water. When the plane's black box was recovered, it was discovered that he had actually been accelerating toward the ocean, erroneously assuming he'd been climbing in altitude.

When everything in the environment is changing, it is impossible to effectively manage the circumstances, especially over the long term. Something must be constant or immovable in order for us to navigate change effectively. If we are sitting in the middle of one of the Great Lakes on a dark, cloudy night and asked to point north, we have a very low probability of getting it right. Something must be stable and constant (e.g., the stars or the shore) in order to navigate.

What, then, does not change in the long run? How can we navigate VUCA environments? Many things remain constant over time, of course, but one of the most important and universally consistent factors is the human inclination toward positive energy. In nature, the sun is a source of life-giving energy. If we put a plant in the window, over time it will lean toward the light. This is an example of the *heliotropic effect*. It is most accurately described this way: All living systems are inclined toward or attracted to that which is life-giving—toward positive energy—and are disinclined toward or avoid that which is life-depleting or life-endangering. All human beings flourish in the presence of positive energy and languish in the presence of negative energy, or they orient themselves toward that which is life-giving and away from that which is life-depleting.[1]

In nature, positive energy is most often experienced in the form of sunlight—photosynthesis occurs only in the presence of light—but positive energy may occur in other forms as well (e.g., interpersonal kindness, high-quality connections, virtuous actions).[2] Logically this makes sense. If we consider evolutionary processes, we observe that every species over time is attracted to that which enhances life and avoids or is repelled by that which diminishes or detracts from life.

This principle has enormous implications. It affects the way we rear our children, the type of incentive systems we put in place in our organizations, the kinds of relationships we form with our employees and acquaintances, and the behaviors we demonstrate in turbulent and trying times. Because it is universal and unwavering, the heliotropic effect provides a constant anchor by which we can navigate changing conditions.

The remainder of this chapter provides an explanation of the heliotropic effect and some of the empirical evidence that confirms its importance and universality in human beings. The concept of positive energy, and, in particular, the kind of energy that is associated with effective leadership, is then explained.

THE HELIOTROPIC EFFECT

The *heliotropic* effect and the *phototropic* effect are similar. Both describe a tendency of all living things to orient themselves toward light—or toward life-giving energy. Einstein equated light and energy by stating that light is simply nature's way of transferring energy through space.[3] Florence Nightingale famously stated, "It is the unqualified result of all my experience with the sick, that second only to their need for fresh air is their need of light . . . and it is not only light but direct sun-light that they want. . . . People think that the effect is upon their spirits only. This is by no means the case. The sun is not only a painter but a sculptor."[4] Abundant scientific evidence confirms that human beings orient themselves toward light and that light provides life-giving energy.

This empirical evidence comes from a variety of sources. The phenomenon was first studied in 1832 by A.P. de Candolle and then by Charles Darwin and George John Romanes in the 1890s. They limited their studies primarily to plants and mammals.[5] Studies of insects as well as a wide variety of forms of animal life subsequently demonstrated that these species also universally orient themselves toward light.[6] This tendency is explained by an innate photochemical reaction that exists in living creatures at the cellular level.[7]

For example, when light enters the eye and hits the retina and the rod and cone cells within it, the light is converted to electrical energy, which produces a visual experience.[8] This energy is transmitted to cells in the brain called the suprachiasmatic nucleus (SNC), which regulates our biological clock. The SNC is part of the hypothalamus, and together they regulate hunger, thirst, sleep, hormones, and the nervous system.[9]

Light turns on chemical reactions within all living organisms, and so our bodies are dependent on light for life-giving energy.[10] These same sensitivities to light exist within the individual cells and proteins in our own bodies. Research has shown that our bodies are filled with numerous light-sensitive chemical switches and amplifiers.[11] Even single-cell organisms without eyes have light-sensitive molecules on their outer membranes that supply them with energy. Human encounters with light, however, are more than skin-deep, and the human body is not a darkened cavern. Instead, light plays an important role within the body.

For example, cytochrome explains how lasers can heal so many different conditions. Cytochrome converts light from the sun into energy for the cells. Most of the photons are absorbed by the energy powerhouses within the cells—the mitochondria—so that as the sun's photons pass through the membranes and come in contact with the cytochrome, they are absorbed and stimulate the creation of a molecule that stores energy in our cells. This molecule, called ATP (adenosine triphosphate), is like a battery, providing energy for the cell's work. ATP can also provide energy that is used by the immune systems and for cellular repair, increase the use of oxygen, improve blood circulation, and stimulate the growth of new blood vessels.[12]

Michael Hamblin at the Harvard Medical School has produced scores of studies showing how light not only produces life-giving energy for the body but also can be used to destroy cancer cells, repair athletic injuries, overcome traumatic brain injury, treat dementia, and promote significant wound healing.[13]

This relationship between light and the heliotropic effect was known by the ancients, and Egyptian, Greek, Indian, and Buddhist healers all used systematic exposure to the sun to foster healing. It was rediscovered in 2005, for example, that putting patients recovering from surgery in a sunlit room (as opposed to an artificially lit room) significantly decreased their pain. Exposure to full-spectrum light was found to be as effective as medication for some depressed patients, with fewer side effects.[14]

Moreover, light has been found to be the key factor in regulating the human body's circadian system, or the internal clock that keeps the body synchronized with the 24-hour solar day. The circadian system is responsible for a range of bodily functions and for regulating key hormones, including those that control sleep (melatonin), hunger (leptin), and the ability to feel satiated (grenhlin). Disrupted circadian rhythms lead to poor sleep and to a variety of diseases such as obesity, diabetes, heart disease, and a number of cancers.[15] Physiologically speaking, evidence suggests that human beings are dependent on and are inherently inclined toward light and toward the resultant positive energy to thrive. The heliotropic effect explains why human beings are so affected by positive energy.

FORMS OF ENERGY

In addition to its connection with light, positive energy is also a product of other sources. My colleague Wayne

Baker has published an excellent summary of the energy literature in which he discusses several different kinds of energy.[16] Energy, he suggests, has been used synonymously with a variety of similar concepts such as arousal, positive affect, zest, and vitality. He indicates that in physics, biology, and chemistry, energy is defined as the capacity to do work, and this designation has been applied to human behavior as well. Energy has traditionally been equated with the capacity to do work.

Colleagues Ryan Quinn, Gretchen Spreitzer, and Chak Fu Lam differentiated the capacity to do work, however, from another form of energy that is not necessarily related to taking action.[17] They classified energy as being in one of two forms: (1) *activation potential,* or the capacity to do work, and (2) *energetic stimulation,* or the feeling of aliveness, enthusiasm, and vitality.

The first form of energy—activation potential—is associated with the amount of glucose/glycogen and ATP in the body.[18] This form of energy is a resource that may be increased or depleted. A great deal of advertising, for example, focuses on helping people feel more energized by working out on exercise equipment, eating a healthy diet, losing weight, taking nutritional supplements, and so forth. Usually, this form of energy diminishes as it is expended. Someone who runs a marathon will become fatigued and will need recovery time. Physical energy wanes.

Similarly, someone who engages in an argument, cheers at an athletic contest, or gets reprimanded by a boss will deplete his or her *emotional energy*. A break is most often needed in order to recover. Emotional energy is reduced with its expenditure over time.

Someone who studies all weekend for an exam, intensely concentrates on memorizing difficult material, and works to figure out a complex computational problem will become exhausted and will need some time to recuperate. *Mental energy* diminishes over time with use. Each of these types of energy—physical, emotional, and mental—is an example of the first form of energy: activation potential. They are resources that diminish with use because glucose/glycogen and ATP become depleted as they are expended.

The second form of energy—energetic stimulation—is not an accumulated resource but a state of being or a feeling of affective arousal. It is experienced as inspired emotions and positive feelings.[19] *Relational energy* is an example of this second form of energy. Relational energy refers to the energy that is associated with interpersonal interactions. Unlike other forms of energy, it usually elevates or intensifies when it is exhibited. For example, we seldom become exhausted by being around people with whom we have loving, supportive relationships. We are seldom, if ever, depleted by people with whom we have trusting, caring, tender connections. In fact, we often seek out individuals who love us and whom we love in order to become renewed and energized. In other words, relational energy is self-enhancing and self-renewing.

A variety of studies demonstrate that experiencing positive relational energy lengthens life, and that people are two to four times more likely to die at an earlier age if they do not consistently experience relational energy.[20] Positive relational energy is a better predictor of long-term health and mortality than factors such as smoking, excessive drinking, and obesity.[21]

Employees' performance at work is also significantly enhanced by relational energy because individuals are more likely to seek out and share information and resources with positive energizers. Positive relational energy is also effective in increasing the performance of individual employees when it is demonstrated by leaders.[22] In addition, it is the kind of energy that differentiates especially effective leaders from others. Successful leaders are almost always positive energizers.

One reason positive relational energy is so important for leaders is aptly described by a friend, Toshi Harada, who serves as a senior executive in the world's largest wheel manufacturer. Toshi is a strong advocate of positive relational energy in leadership. Here is his explanation of its importance:

> One of the basics of Japanese manufacturing principles is to eliminate or minimize the waste in the manufacturing process. What I'm finding is that negatively energizing leaders are creating significant waste in the organization. For example, think of a traveler on the street in the winter of Michigan. If a cold wind blows to the traveler, he wears more clothes on [sic]. And, when negative leaders try to create results by pointing out the weaknesses of the people and rely on punishment, a similar thing happens. People are going to close their

minds. So, negatively energizing leaders can reach some short-term results. But when the team members close their minds, those short-term oriented results cannot be sustained. So it's going to be a roller coaster—up and down, up and down. In order for us to have long-term sustaining improvement, we really need to have positive energizing leaders.[23]

Positive energy, in other words, is both efficient and effective in producing desirable results when demonstrated by leaders.

Individuals do not express these various types of energy in a completely independent way, of course. In many activities, individuals may demonstrate several kinds of energy at the same time. A caregiver who homeschools and organizes activities for children all day during a COVID-19 isolation period, for example, may find these tasks physically and emotionally exhausting. More than one kind of energy will be expended and diminished at the same time. However, when these same children snuggle up for a bedtime story at the end of the day, the elevation in relational energy creates renewal. Relational energy is a self-enhancing energetic stimulation.

ENERGY, INFLUENCE, EXTROVERSION, AND INTRINSIC MOTIVATION

In the scholarly literature, positive energy is sometimes confused with other concepts such as influence, extroversion, or intrinsic motivation.[24] Important differences exist, however, among these various concepts. For instance, influence is usually defined in terms of the ability to get other people to do or believe what you want them to do or believe.[25] The vast majority of the leadership literature equates leadership and influence. If you are influential, it means you are a leader. People will follow others who are influential. The difference between influence and energy, however, can be illustrated by a situation in which two individuals are influential and two individuals are positive energizers.

When two highly influential people disagree, the likely consequence is conflict. Both will want to influence the other. Of the more than 40 wars currently being fought on the planet, all are, essentially, struggles to determine who will be in control or who is the most influential. Differences among influencers will almost always lead to competition or conflict. Managing the dynamics associated with influence, therefore, is almost always similar to managing power, conflict, or rivalry.

On the other hand, when two people who are positive energizers disagree, the consequence will be quite different. Because positive energy is heliotropic, the two individuals are much more likely to work together or try to interact more frequently. Positive energy attracts them to one another rather than having them strive to be in control of the other or to be the person in charge. Interactions and attempts at collaboration will most likely increase. Managing positive energizers in an organization, therefore, is quite different from managing influencers. Managing energy is more likely to focus on facilitating collaboration. Managing influence is more likely to focus on conflict resolution.

Positive energy is also sometimes confused with extroversion. Extroverts are individuals who are outgoing, talkative, social, and lively. The opposite of an extrovert is an introvert—someone who is quiet, reserved, calm, and passive. Energizers are often merely seen as the extroverts in the room and difficult not to notice.

Empirical evidence suggests, however, that extroversion and positive energy are not the same. Extroversion is only slightly related to individual well-being and personal satisfaction, for example, unless accompanied by positive energy. In fact, the correlation between extroversion and positive relational energy is very low and nonsignificant.[26] Positive energy is strongly related to well-being. Extroverts can be dominating and exhausting rather than energizing and uplifting. They can merely take up time and attention while not helping other people feel energized at all. The research indicates, in fact, that when extroverts are also positive energizers, the correlation with well-being and personal satisfaction is very strong. This is not the case when positive energy is absent.[27]

We all know individuals who are not the first to speak, not out front in every activity, or not clamoring for attention but who give life to the system, uplift others around them, and are described as more introverted than extroverted. Positively energizing people are not the same as extroverted people, because positive energy is not a personality variable. Introverted people can be as positively energizing as extroverts.

Some have also assumed that positive energy is merely intrinsic motivation. This concept refers to a desire to act without the pursuit of an external reward or recognition.[28] Intrinsically motivated individuals are driven by an internal sense of satisfaction, meaningfulness, or learning. Intrinsically motivated people pursue goals merely to attain a sense of achievement. Extrinsically motivated individuals pursue goals to obtain a reward or recognition from others. They rely on an external incentive to motivate their effort.

Positive energy—particularly positive relational energy—is not a product of motivational forces but refers to the extent to which a relationship is elevating, uplifting, and enriching. So, positive relational energy is both a social phenomenon and an individual phenomenon: it is social in that it results from relationships, and it is personal in that it is experienced as an internal feeling or sentiment. Positive energy is not a motivational drive but a condition at which individuals arrive. It results from human connection, not the presence or absence of a reward. Positive energy may or may not be associated with meaningfulness, which is a key attribute of intrinsic motivation.

CONCLUSION

A key purpose of this book is to identify ways to help leaders increase and enhance positive relational energy. Abundant scientific research makes a compelling case that the most effective leaders, and the leaders who best demonstrate positively energizing practices, produce extraordinarily high performance in their organizations and in their employees. Displaying positive energy produces high levels of performance in organizations because employees tend to be more engaged in their work, are more likely to associate their work with a sense of calling, are more likely to experience personal well-being, and are more likely to display innovation and extra-mile discretionary effort at work.[29] In schools, students whose teachers display positive relational energy experience more academic gains than students whose teachers do not display this energy.[30]

The chapters that follow explain how these outcomes occur, how to foster positive relational energy, and how positive energy has been used to produce extraordinarily successful performance in a variety of organizational settings, especially in times characterized by VUCA conditions.

2
POSITIVE ENERGY
IN ORGANIZATIONS

This chapter helps elaborate the concept of positive relational energy and highlights the effects of positive relational energy in leaders. It shows how positively energizing leaders affect employees and the success of their organizations. It also discusses how we can identify positive energizers and what to look for if we want to hire them in our organizations.

POSITIVE ENERGY AND LEADERSHIP

A common way to identify leadership in organizations is by examining an organizational chart. Individuals occupying boxes near the top of the chart are likely to be designated as the leaders—they are held accountable for the organization's performance, strategy, and fiscal health. Leadership is often equated with responsibility for outcomes. Figure 2.1, for example, shows a traditional organization chart. The lines connecting the boxes show

I am indebted to my colleague Wayne Baker for introducing the concept of positive energy networks discussed in this chapter.

FIGURE 2.1

A traditional hierarchical organization chart

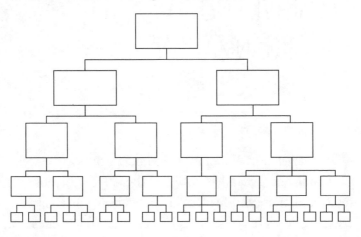

who reports to whom and who resides in the most senior positions. We have all seen these kinds of charts because they are a common way to identify who the leaders are.

Some alternatives exist for depicting the positions of people in organizations, however, and the most common is called a network map. We have all seen a network map in the back of an airline magazine. Cities are connected with airline routes, so some cities are shown at the hub and some are on the periphery in the map. In an organization network map, people rather than cities are the nodes.

So, how do we use a network map to identify leaders?

One of the most common ways to identify leaders is to construct a network map based on information flows. The relevant question is, Who gives information to whom, and who gets information from whom? The research on network analysis is very clear: if you are at the center or hub of an information network, not only are you seen as a leader but your performance is higher than the norm, as is the performance of the unit you manage.[1] This makes sense. If all of the information flows through you, you can decide what to share, you know all the secrets, you control the messages, and therefore you have an advantage. Your performance will likely exceed others' performance, and the unit you manage will surpass other units' performance as well.

A common alternative to examining an organization's information network is to examine its influence network. The relevant question is, Who influences whom, and who is influenced by whom? Again, the results of research are not surprising. If you are at the center or hub of an influence network, you are likely to be viewed as the leader. Moreover, your performance will be higher than the average, as will the performance of the unit you manage.[2] Again, these results make sense. If you can get people to follow you, if you can influence their goals and objectives, if you can wield power over others, and if you get your way most of the time, you will have an advantage and your performance will exceed that of others.

In the academic and popular literature, influence is by far the most dominant attribute of leadership. In fact, it is almost always equated with being the leader.[3] The standard assumption is that if you are influential, you are a leader. Leaders influence others. Followers follow because they are influenced by leaders.

My colleagues and I have found, however, that there is an alternative to influence as the chief indicator of effective leadership. This alternative has to do with positive energy, especially positive relational energy.[4] So, how can we identify positive relational energy?

We can assess this kind of energy by asking the question, Who gives energy to whom, and who receives energy from whom? In the same way we measured information and influence networks, we can create a positive energy network map in an organization quite easily. We use the same method but ask each person to respond to the question, When I interact with this person, what happens to my energy? To what extent am I enthused, elevated, and uplifted when I interact with this person?

Note that we are not asking people to rate another person's energy. Rather, we ask individuals to rate the energy in the relationship. A 7-point scale is used to rate one's interactions with another person. For example, a 1 would indicate "I am very de-energized when I interact with this person," a 4 would indicate "I am neither energized nor de-energized when I interact with this person," and a 7 would indicate "I am very positively energized when I interact with this person."

Having each person rate his or her energizing connection with every other person in the group produces a set of ratings associated with each person's name. These ratings are entered into a network mapping statistical program (there are many available online), and the program creates a network map based on relational energy—that is, the energy exchanged when two people interact. We

FIGURE 2.2

A positive energy network

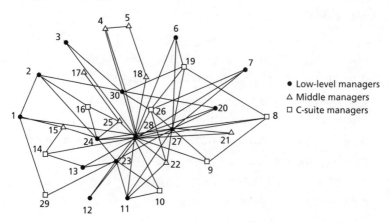

can easily determine who the positive energizers are (the nodes or hubs in the network), who the de-energizers are, and who is on the periphery and has few energizing connections. Figure 2.2 shows such a network.

As it turns out, energy is more powerful in accounting for the performance of employees and of the organization than are influence, information, and most other motivators used to induce high performance. This evidence is summarized below.

THE IMPORTANCE OF POSITIVE RELATIONAL ENERGY

As mentioned in chapter 1, several kinds of energy can be identified—physical energy, emotional energy, and mental energy, which, over time, diminish with use. Relational energy is the only kind of energy that elevates or increases with use. Experiencing relational energy renews and uplifts us in the process of interacting with other people.

Figure 2.2 displays the positive energy network map of the managers in a large international retail firm. Each point (a dot, triangle, or square) represents a person who is rated by others on a 7-point Likert scale on the basis of the extent to which interacting with this person is positively energizing or not. The lines show who is receiving positive energy from others and who is giving positive energy to others. A rating of 6 or 7 means that a person is highly positively energizing.

The squares represent the C-suite employees or the most senior-level leaders. The triangles represent middle managers. The dots are the most junior people or those at the bottom of the hierarchy. Notice that there are several people at the senior level (squares) who energize hardly anyone (for example, numbers 8, 9, 10, and 29 in the network). They are positively energizing very few people in the organization and, one would assume, are not earning their multimillion-dollar compensation packages.

On the other hand, look at the middle of the network and you will find several junior-level people (dots) who are giving life to this organization. That is, these junior-level people are positively energizing many others and are providing an uplift to the organization (for example, numbers 27, 28, and 30); they are also receiving positive energy from many others. The point is, a person's position in the organization's hierarchy and the extent to which he or she is a positive energizer are not related.

FIGURE 2.3

A de-energizing network

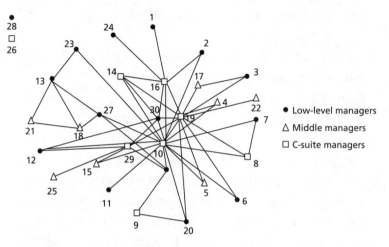

Whether the person is the CEO or a new analyst, a general or a corporal, a professor or a graduate student does not matter; hierarchical position is not predictive of positive energy.

Figure 2.3 shows the de-energizing network in the same organization. These people are rated as a 1 or 2 on the 7-point Likert scale. They are de-energizing others—sucking the life out of the system—and producing negative relational energy. As you can see, several senior-level people (squares) are de-energizing many other employees (for example, numbers 10, 16, 19, and 29) and diminishing others in their interactions.

In the upper-left corner of the network map are two people (numbers 26 and 28) who do not de-energize anyone. No one rates either person as a 1 or 2 on the Likert scale. These two people, however, are the only employees in the organization with no negative ratings. The implication is that most people are not merely energizers or de-energizers. Rather, most people energize some people and de-energize others. Energizing is not an all-or-nothing condition. In fact, a similar ratio exists with positive communication and energizing. If you energize three to five more people than you de-energize, you have an overall positive, energizing effect on the organization.[5]

In another organization I studied, almost all of the senior managers were rated by employees as de-energizers. A majority of people in senior-level positions were given a 1 or 2 rating in the survey of interactions. After being shown these data, the company, to its credit, announced the initiation of a program to develop positively energizing leadership among its senior managers.

The most important point is that positive energy is a set of behaviors that can be developed. Positive energy is not just personal charisma. It is not just extroversion or a personality dimension. It is not just physical attractiveness. Positive energy is defined by a set of behaviors that anyone can learn and develop. Some key attributes of positive energy and some suggestions for how to develop positively energizing leadership are provided in chapters 3 and 4.

Figure 2.4 shows an information sharing or communication network constructed by my colleague Rob Cross.[6] The network map shows who gives information to whom and who gets information from whom. You can see that many communication lines are well used. A lot of information sharing is taking place. Figure 2.5 shows

FIGURE 2.4

An information sharing network

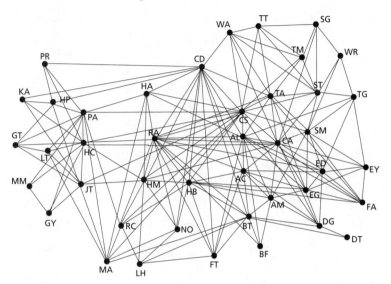

Source: Used with permission of Rob Cross.

the same information sharing network among the de-energizers. Communication barely exists. That is, people tend not to communicate or interact with people who are de-energizing because the emotional and social costs are so high. It's exhausting to interact with de-energizers. The statistical relationship between communication and energy, therefore, is positive: the more positive energy, the greater the communication. Both frequency and richness of information sharing increase among positively energizing connections.

It is also possible to identify the density of an energy network. Density is measured by examining the connections between all possible members of a group

FIGURE 2.5

Information sharing among de-energizers

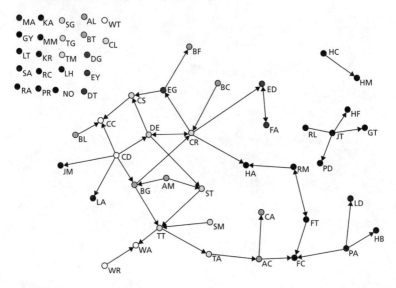

or organization. The question is, Of all possible pair-wise connections, how many are positively energizing and how many are de-energizing? When every single person rates every other person in terms of energy, how many of those connections are rated as positively energizing? As may be expected, the denser the positive energy network—that is, the more every person in the network positively energizes every other person in the network—the higher the performance of the organization. Everyone can, in other words, create a positively energizing relationship with other people.[7]

Everyone cannot be the most influential person in an organization, of course, nor can everyone be the center or hub of an information network. Information and influence resources are limited. On the other hand, everyone can be a positive energizer, not just those occupying senior positions. Any interpersonal connection can become energizing; thus, positive energy is a non-zero-sum game. It can be infinitely expanded in a system.

POSITIVE ENERGY AND PERFORMANCE

Three important conclusions have emerged from research on positive energy in organizations. The first is that *people who are positive energizers are higher performers than others*. This is not surprising. People who tend to uplift and give life to others are likely to perform better than people who do not. There is a surprise finding, however, that has emerged from my own and my colleague Wayne Baker's research: a person's position in the positive energy network is significantly more important in predicting performance than a person's position in the information or influence network. Energy is substantially more important in accounting for individual performance, and for a unit's performance, than is information or influence.[8]

What is important about this finding is that almost all leaders in organizations constantly manage information: "Did you go to the meeting?" "Did you get the memo?" "Do you understand our strategy?" "Are you informed about what we want to get done?" Similarly, managing influence is a critical part of the job of leaders: "Here are the incentives." "Here are the goals." "Will you respond to the pressure to meet our targets?"

However, an important question is, Is positive energy ever managed, or managed to the same extent as is information or influence, by leaders? Do people ever get recognized or rewarded or hired or promoted because they are positive energizers? Usually not, because energy is seldom recognized as an important resource. Empirical evidence suggests, however, that energy should get priority because it is substantially more important than what normally receives leaders' attention.

A second conclusion is that *positive energizers impact the performance of those with whom they interact.*[9] That is, positive energizers account for an inordinate amount of performance because other people tend to flourish in their presence. The heliotropic effect helps explain why. People flourish in the presence of positive energy or life-giving influences. In professional athletic organizations, for example, we have all noticed that teams often trade for players who may be past their peak years of performance but who are needed for the clubhouse. It is well known in professional sports that positive energizers in the locker room can account for team wins that would otherwise not be achieved. This is because positive energizers affect the performance of individuals with whom they interact.

A good example is a friend, Shane Battier, who was drafted into the National Basketball Association (NBA) in 2001. Shane was Player of the Year in high school, was Player of the Year in college, and then played for three teams in the NBA before his retirement in 2014. Battier's personal statistics were not spectacular as a player, and the media often labeled him as a midlevel player without the needed physical skills to be great. On the other hand, every time Battier was hired by a new team, that team won at least 20 more games than the previous year and made the playoffs. Battier made the NBA finals three times and won twice. One analyst, reviewing Battier's career, summarized it this way:

> When he is on the court, his teammates get better, often a lot better, and his opponents get worse—often a lot worse. He may not grab huge numbers of rebounds, but he has the uncanny ability to improve his teammates' rebounding. He doesn't shoot much, but when he does, he takes only the most efficient shots. He also has a knack for getting the ball to teammates who are in position to do the same, and he commits few turnovers. On defense, although he routinely guards the NBA's most prolific scorers, he significantly reduces their shooting percentages. At the same time, he somehow improves the defensive efficiency of his teammates . . . helping his team in all sorts of subtle hard-to-measure ways that appear to violate his own personal interests.[10]

Battier simply helped other teammates perform better on the court than they would have otherwise—a good example of the second conclusion.

A third major conclusion from empirical research is that *highly performing organizations have many more positive energizers than normal organizations—as many as three times more.* Positive energizers can reside throughout the organization at any hierarchical level.

Anyone can learn to display the attributes of a positive energizer, and because performance is so highly dependent on positive energizers, organizations need more of them. Moreover, because positive energy is not a personality trait but rather a set of behavioral attributes, training in the enhancement of positive energy should be an important part of the leadership development agenda. A growing number of organizations have found this energizing development strategy to be highly effective in producing above-average bottom-line performance. (Chapter 4 addresses the development of positively energizing leadership.)

It is true that short-term results can be achieved by de-energizing leaders or individuals who deplete and diminish other people. Several well-known leaders in highly recognized organizations seem to have achieved high levels of success without being positively energizing to those around them. But, in the long run, and as pointed out by Toshi Harada in chapter 1, inefficiencies, protective behaviors, wasted energy, diminished information flows, lower levels of innovation, less psychological safety, and increased defensiveness will mitigate the level of performance that could have been achieved in the presence of positive energy. The research is clear that positive energy matters a lot, and it especially matters in leaders.

Figure 2.6 reports the results of one particular study my colleagues and I conducted with more than 200 employees who rated the positive energy they experienced when they interacted with the leader of their own organizations. A five-item scale was used:

FIGURE 2.6

Impact of positively energizing leaders on employees

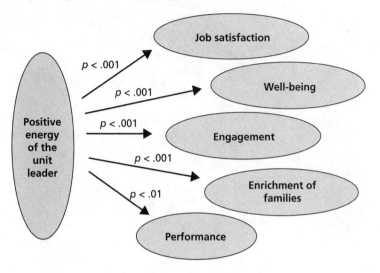

- *I feel invigorated when I interact with this person.*
- *After interacting with this person I feel more energy to do my work.*
- *I feel increased vitality when I interact with this person.*
- *I would go to this person when I need to be "pepped up."*
- *After an exchange with this person I feel more stamina to do my work.*

The results demonstrate the effects of positively energizing leaders on their employees' job satisfaction, well-being, engagement, and performance. The arrows labeled with "$p < .001$" indicate that the probability that this relationship occurs by chance is less than 1 in

FIGURE 2.7

Impact of positively energizing leaders on the organization

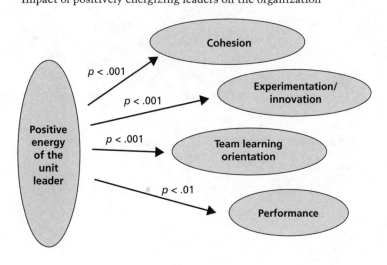

1,000—that is, there is a very strong relationship between the positive energy demonstrated by the unit leader and the outcomes on the right side of the figure. Employees' job satisfaction, well-being, engagement, and performance are higher when their leader is a positive energizer. One surprising finding was that enrichment of families, or family well-being, is also significantly affected by the positive energy of the work unit leader. Positively energizing leaders had an impact outside the work setting itself, especially on employees' families.[11]

In addition, figure 2.7 shows the effects of the energizing leader on the performance of the organization itself. Not only were individuals affected by the leader's energy, but the bottom-line performance, learning orientation, experimentation and innovation, and cohesion of the organization all were significantly enhanced when they experienced a positively energizing leader.

Knowing that positive energy is an important resource to be managed in organizations, and being convinced that positively energizing leaders have a significant impact on employees and on bottom-line performance, leads us to ask two important questions: How can we identify the positive energizers in our team or organization? What do we look for if we want to hire more positive energizers?

IDENTIFYING POSITIVE ENERGIZERS

On several occasions I have been invited to help senior executives identify the positive energizers in their organizations. This process can often be useful when a senior executive takes on a new role and does not have a history with his or her subordinates. Knowing who the positive energizers are, and who tends to be de-energizing, is a real advantage to a new leader. At least three options exist for helping to identify the positive energizers within a management team.

One option, and the most accurate one, is to ask each person on the management team to rate the relational energy they experience with every other member of the team on a 7-point scale (where 1 is very de-energizing and 7 is very positively energizing). A data matrix will result with ratings associated with every person. A network map[12] is created using readily available network mapping software. A variation of figure 2.2 (shown earlier) will result.

A second option is illustrated by a senior executive of a worldwide retail firm who was interested in creating a network map of his top 40 executives. He was new to the role and eager to identify the energizers in his leadership team. We began by asking each member of his 40-person team to rate the other 39 members. However, within an hour of distributing the request, he received phone calls from several of his team members. They indicated that they were happy to do the ratings but wanted them to be confidential. They did not want other team members to know how the relationship was being rated.

This, of course, eliminates the possibility of creating a network map, because there is no way to draw lines between two anonymous individuals. A second option was used, therefore, to identify the positive energizers in the top team.

Each of the top 40 people still rated each other member of the team, but feedback to the entire leadership team and to each individual showed just the number of individuals who were rated as 6 and 7 (indicating highly energizing relationships) as well as the number who were rated as 1 and 2 (indicating de-energizing relationships). Figures 2.8 and 2.9 show the results of the ratings.

In figure 2.8, each bubble represents a member of the top management team, and the number within each bubble is how many times that person was rated by others as highly energizing (6 or 7). One person was rated

FIGURE 2.8

The positively energizing leaders

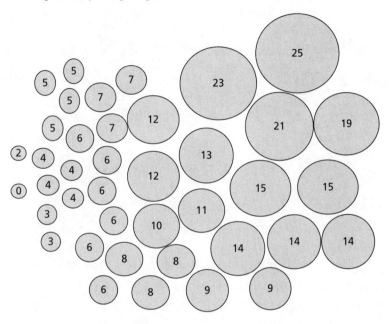

by 25 other team members as being positively energizing, one person had 23 nominations, one had 21 nominations, and so forth. One member of the top team received no ratings of positively energizing. In figure 2.9, 9 members of the team had no one rate them as deenergizing, but one person had 13 nominations as a deenergizer, one had 9 nominations, two had 8 nominations, and so forth.

These data were shared in an anonymous fashion with the entire team of 40, and each individual was given his or her own data. Each person also had a chance to receive one-to-one coaching regarding his or her ratings

FIGURE 2.9

The de-energizing leaders

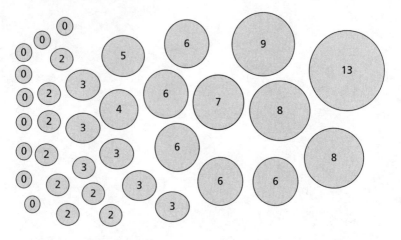

to assist with interpretation and to help provide developmental opportunities if desired. The CEO received all the data, including the individual ratings of each person.

The value of this information for the CEO included his ability to more fully and more accurately identify the energizers and the de-energizers in his top team and to provide developmental experiences to enhance the density of the network. He was able to mobilize the positively energizing members of his team to help lead change initiatives and foster commitment to his strategic plan. He was also able to identify those who were likely to generate resistance and/or who needed to be coached to become more valued members of his team. (Chapter 4 also discusses action implications for these kinds of data.)

This second option for identifying positive energizers is known as a "bubble chart" and can be readily performed in a short amount of time. Simply ask all members of the group to name the two most positively energizing people in the group, either by writing the names on a slip of paper or by emailing the names to you. Count the number of nominations each person receives. A bubble chart is an easy way to display the results anonymously. It allows the leader to learn who the most positively energizing people in the group are, and the group gets a general sense of the energy network in the room. These data can be collected in 10 minutes in real time.

A third option is a pulse survey. Some CEOs send a weekly email to their employees asking this question: On a scale of 1 to 10, what is your energy today? If the Tokyo office previously averaged 9.3 and it is now at 7.8, the CEO shows up to help diagnose issues and boost the group's energy. The energy of employees is monitored on a weekly basis using a one-question email so that a picture of the collective energy of a group can be examined.

HIRING POSITIVE ENERGIZERS

If we need to supplement our current team or organization with more positively energizing people, what do we look for? What kinds of questions could we ask to find positive energizers to hire? These questions can be addressed by using an example close to home.

The Department of Management and Organizations at the University of Michigan has been rated among the top management departments in the world for the past decade or so.[13] One key reason for this ranking is the criteria used to hire faculty members. Three criteria dominate the selection process. First, a candidate has to be a world-class scholar. His or her research has to make an important scholarly contribution to the discipline. This is no surprise, because producing scholarship is the key role of a research university. Everyone wants world-class scholars.

Second, a candidate must be a good teacher. He or she has to make a difference in students' lives by the content and pedagogy used in the classroom. This criterion is also no surprise. All world-class universities seek candidates who excel in the classroom and in their scholarship.

The third criterion is the differentiator for the department. The candidate must be a net-positive energizer. This means that candidates must add more positive energy to the system than they extract. No one can be a positive energizer all the time, of course, but the balance has to be in favor of positively energizing other people. This eliminates self-aggrandizing curmudgeons, people who care only about themselves, people who compete to make certain they get the credit, and people who are not willing to invest in their colleagues. The result, over the past 15 years, is that each faculty member in the department invests in and genuinely supports the 15 other people in the department. Each department member is actively committed to helping other department members get better every day. Each faculty member is being positively energized by their colleagues much of the time.

A question that remains, of course, is how to find people to hire who are positive energizers. How can we identify a positively energizing candidate? When the individual is not familiar, how can we know?

One approach is to conduct an interview with the candidate in which specific questions are asked that reveal positive energizing. An example of questions I prefer was adapted from Laura Queen, vice president of organization development and chief development officer at G&W Laboratories. Her questions have been modified, but they illustrate the approach taken to identify positively energizing candidates.

- *Describe a role you've had that you absolutely loved. Describe why you fell in love with it. What did you learn?*
- *Describe an organization you've worked for that you've fallen in love with. What was it about this organization that caused you to love it? What did you learn?*
- *Describe a project, a work experience, or a challenging situation that exemplifies when you have done your best work. Describe this situation or challenge. What contributed to your success? What did you*

learn? If you could do it all over again, what would you do differently?

- *Describe the best leadership or management team you've ever been a part of. What made this team so special? What did you learn?*
- *Describe the best leader you've worked with or worked for. What made this leader so special? What did you learn from this person? What is one gift from this person that you carry with you today?*
- *Describe a situation in which a coworker or employee needed your assistance to succeed or flourish. How did you help this person achieve his or her highest potential? What did you learn?*
- *Describe a time when you achieved peak performance, when you have been at your best, or when you have become positively deviant. What did you do? What did you learn?*

Many people have a difficult time answering these questions. They have never been in love with any organization or any role. They have never reached peak performance themselves. They have never helped anyone else flourish and reach their highest potential. They have never learned the lessons that are associated with positively deviant performance and positively energizing experiences. They have never been a positive energizer that affected the life of a colleague. These questions help identify individuals who have experienced positive energy and demonstrated it with others.

DIVERSITY, EQUITY, AND INCLUSION

Understandably, some may dismiss these questions as irrelevant in the face of current concerns related to diversity, equity, and inclusion. Class-action lawsuits, boycotts, civil unrest, and lost employment have intensified concerns about these issues, so some individuals may dismiss a focus on virtuousness and positive relational energy as being irrelevant to their current concerns. Accusations of injustice, privilege, unconscious bias, and systemic racism are, appropriately, receiving a great deal of attention, and questions regarding falling in love with an organization or role, reaching one's highest potential, or helping someone else flourish may seem beside the point.

At least three approaches have been applied to the concern with improving diversity, equity, and inclusion. One common response is to approach the issue as a demographic problem. The rationale is that it is important to ensure that positions of status, membership, and privilege have representatives from multiple demographic groups. These groups are usually defined on the basis of ethnicity, skin color, gender, personal preferences, handicaps, and so forth. Sometimes formal or informal quotas are used to ensure that demographic diversity and inclusion in organizations occur.

There are distinct advantages of this approach, including ensuring access to higher economic and status positions for traditionally underrepresented groups and opening doors of opportunity for people who may be disadvantaged as a result of their demographic characteristics. In addition, bringing diverse individuals together may help increase understanding, empathy, and innovativeness, which can develop when heterogeneous groups work together.[14]

A second common response to concerns with diversity, equity, and inclusion is to offer sensitivity training or consciousness-raising education. Helping individuals become aware of their unconscious biases and the barriers faced by underrepresented minorities helps increase understanding and empathy and, hopefully, can lead to policy and behavioral changes. The advantages of this kind of training include an elevated awareness both in individuals and in organizations of the systemic biases and the behaviors that may be offensive to various individuals or groups and that keep them down. These training sessions may also create more cohesive and connected relationships among diverse individuals.

A common concern with these two approaches is that they often do not produce the intended outcomes. One study of 829 firms over three decades found that these approaches actually make things worse, not better.[15] Merely putting people together geographically or involving them in awareness-enhancing sessions does not guarantee that behavior will change and that ingrained or systemic bias will be mitigated. Creating demographic quotas and pointing out offensive behavior have often been criticized as ineffective in achieving genuine diversity, equity, and inclusion.

A third approach centers on positively energizing leadership, particularly the demonstration of virtuous behaviors. Individuals who demonstrate generosity, compassion, gratitude, trustworthiness, forgiveness, and kindness toward others are positively energized and renewed. Virtuousness is heliotropic. Virtuous actions produce positive relational energy, so the probability of forming unbiased, authentic, supportive relationships is enhanced. Virtuousness is, by definition, absent motives of recognition, reward, or payback. Virtuous actions are genuine and expressed for their own inherent value, so recipients of virtuous actions do not feel manipulated or co-opted for other purposes. Unbiased, authentic, supportive relationships are enhanced.

In this third approach, all individuals are encouraged to assist others in fulfilling their highest potential as well as working toward reaching their own potential. Hiring decisions are focused on the extent to which individuals are working to reach their own peak performance as well as helping others achieve their potential rather than emphasizing demographic factors. Virtuousness refers to an aspiration in human beings to reach their highest potential, so when leaders demonstrate virtuous behaviors and seek them in others, other individuals are more likely to flourish—to dream more, learn more, do more, and become more. The barriers endemic in racism, injustice, and systemic bias tend to be minimized and replaced with a focus on the best of the human condition—helping each person fulfill his or her highest aspirations. This is one reason why positively energizing leadership is so crucial in attracting positively energizing people and in creating a culture of diversity, equity, and inclusion.

CONCLUSION

A great deal of evidence is available that confirms that positively energizing leadership and positive practices produce successful performance in organizations. Even in industries that normally eschew practices that are not linked to bottom-line results, positively energizing leadership has been shown to have significant positive impact on performance. The display of positive energy in leaders, in fact, has proved to be much more important in predicting performance than the amount of information or influence leaders possess.

Most importantly, the attributes of positively energizing leaders are learned behaviors to which almost anyone has access. That is, everyone has the potential to be a positively energizing leader. The key attributes and behaviors of positively energizing leaders and their impact on organizational performance are discussed in the following chapter.

3
ATTRIBUTES OF POSITIVELY ENERGIZING LEADERS

Research confirms that positively energizing leaders are vital in affecting the performance of employees and their organizations. Moreover, positive energy is not merely a personality dimension or inherent attribute; rather, it results from behaviors that anyone can learn and develop. Therefore, a few questions will naturally arise: What does one need to develop to become a positively energizing leader? What are the attributes of positive energizers? Who are the positive energizers in my organization?

This chapter highlights key attributes of positively energizing leaders, provides more empirical evidence regarding their importance in affecting organizational performance, and describes some practices and activities that help foster positive energy in leaders.

ATTRIBUTES OF POSITIVELY ENERGIZING LEADERS

A good summary definition of positively energizing leadership is captured by a (slightly modified) statement originally attributed to the sixth president of the United States, John Quincy Adams (1767–1868):

> If your actions inspire others to dream more, learn more, do more, and become more, you are a positively energizing leader.

Positively energizing leaders are not self-aggrandizing, dominant individuals who seek the limelight. They are not always in charge or at the front. They are, rather, individuals who produce growth, development, and improvement among others with whom they interact. They exude a certain kind of light or energy that is uplifting and helps others become their best.

To understand more clearly how Adams's statement is operationalized by leaders, interviews were conducted with hundreds of leaders identified as positive energizers as well as with other individuals regarding their observations of those energizers. The questions centered on which attributes positively energizing leaders display themselves as well as how positive energizing leadership can be enhanced.

These interviews produced a set of attributes that differentiate positively energizing leaders from others. Table 3.1 lists the most commonly identified attributes of positively energizing leaders emerging from the interviews. This is not a comprehensive list, of course, because circumstances and culture may alter what is most effective in certain organizations. Other attributes may be effective in certain circumstances and in diverse cultures. This list is universal enough, however, that it can

TABLE 3.1

Attributes of positively energizing leaders

Energizers	De-energizers
1. Help other people flourish without expecting a payback.	1. Ensure that they themselves get the credit.
2. Express gratitude and humility.	2. Are selfish and resist feedback.
3. Instill confidence and self-efficacy in others.	3. Don't create opportunities for others to be recognized.
4. Smile frequently.	4. Are somber and seldom smile.
5. Forgive weaknesses in others.	5. Induce guilt or shame in others.
6. Invest in developing personal relationships.	6. Don't invest in personal relationships.
7. Share plum assignments and recognize others.	7. Keep the best for themselves.
8. Listen actively and empathetically.	8. Dominate the conversation and assert their ideas.
9. Solve problems.	9. Create problems.
10. Mostly see opportunities.	10. Mostly see roadblocks and are critics.
11. Clarify meaningfulness and inspire others.	11. Are indifferent and uncaring.
12. Are trusting and trustworthy.	12. Are skeptical and lack integrity.
13. Are genuine and authentic.	13. Are superficial and insincere.
14. Motivate others to exceed performance standards.	14. Are satisfied with mediocrity or "good enough."
15. Mobilize positive energizers who can motivate others.	15. Ignore energizers who are eager to help.

guide efforts to develop more positively energizing leadership attributes. None of these 15 attributes was mentioned more often than others in the interviews, so none necessarily predominates above others. The numbering is for reference only and does not imply priority. These items represent the attributes that were most frequently mentioned.

A brief explanation of each of these attributes may help highlight their importance in producing positively energizing leadership. When interacting with other people, positively energizing leaders tend to demonstrate the following attributes:

1. *Help other people flourish without expecting a payback.* Positive energizing is not an exchange relationship. A quid pro quo is not expected or assumed in interactions. Positive energizers contribute altruistically for the benefit of others, without expecting recognition or reward. For example, they may anonymously provide assistance to an employee who is in need or provide coaching and mentoring without expecting acknowledgment or recognition.

2. *Express gratitude and humility.* They acknowledge the contributions of others and express gratitude often and immediately. Publicly thanking others and recognizing their contributions is almost always an expression of humility as well. For example, they may send personal thank-you notes to individuals with whom they work or to the families of their employees.

3. *Instill confidence and self-efficacy in others.* They help others feel valued, competent, talented, and completely capable of succeeding. Others feel important in their presence. For example, they may recognize and highlight the talents or abilities of another person, and they may provide support when missteps occur.

4. *Frequently smile.* This is so simple, but it is the single most noticed attribute of positive energizers. In repose, many people may look like they are angry or sad, so positive energizers make sure to communicate positivity through their facial expressions. For example, when they greet people, they make eye contact and tend to have a pleasant look on their faces.

5. *Forgive weaknesses.* They see mistakes as learning opportunities. They help others overcome blunders rather than negatively judge them or create guilt. For example, they may point out the positive in others' miscues or failures and identify ways to improve without inducing shame.

6. *Are personal and know outside-of-work interests.* They show interest in the whole person, not just the work role. A study at the University of Kansas found that it takes about 50 hours of socializing to progress from an acquaintance to a "casual" friend, an additional 40 hours to become a "real" friend, and a total of 200 hours to become a "close" friend.[1] Positively energizing leaders take time to get past the acquaintance phase, to learn about important aspects of employees' lives outside the work setting,

and to treat individuals as whole people, not just titles or functions. For example, they may keep a notebook on individuals' family members and important personal or family events.

7. *Share plum assignments and recognize others' involvement.* They find ways to involve others, to help them find ways to succeed, and to be acknowledged. They are willing to share the limelight without abrogating their own responsibility to lead. For example, they may provide assignments that help other people stretch and grow as well as publicly recognize them for their effort and for their success.

8. *Listen actively and empathetically.* Rather than being quick to give advice, they sincerely seek to understand, they ask questions, and they give full attention to the other person. They are willing to talk openly and honestly with individuals in face-to-face conversations. For example, they may demonstrate humility in being open to feedback, show sensitivity to personal issues that employees may be facing, and respond compassionately when employees experience hurt or pain.

9. *Solve problems rather than create problems.* They tend to solve problems even before others know there are problems. They anticipate others' needs and respond before being asked. For example, they provide assistance before appeals are made, offer resources that may be needed but not requested, or offer know-how and knowledge that avoids a future problem. They take responsibility for generating results.

10. *Mostly see opportunities.* They tend to be optimistic while being balanced with realism. They find ways to move forward rather than being bogged down in problems or "yeah, buts." They remain hopeful about a successful future. For example, they approach challenges and difficulties with a "yes, and" rather than a "yeah, but."

11. *Tend to inspire and provide meaning.* They clarify a profound purpose in the activities they lead so that others see meaningfulness in the undertakings. They elevate others' views. For example, they may help others see the profound purpose of successful goal accomplishment and the impact that it can have on other people.

12. *Are trusting and trustworthy.* Others trust their sincerity and authenticity as well as their dependability. They hold confidences as sacred. They follow through on their word even if it requires sacrifice. For example, they may give others the benefit of the doubt, react charitably, and, when they make a promise, hold their personal honor as more important than a legal contract.

13. *Are genuine and authentic.* Being positive is not an act, a trick, or a technique. Positive energizers strive to be consistent in their values and behavior. They are willing to be vulnerable with others in demonstrating what is most important to them. For example, they may be willing to acknowledge and appropriately share personal challenges and mistakes, thereby placing themselves in a vulnerable position.

14. *Expect very high performance standards.* They help others exceed expectations. They motivate others to achieve positive deviance and reach their highest potential. They recognize that good performance seldom wins championships, but that great performance is required. For example, they motivate others to achieve more than they thought possible and to reach a potential that they did not know they possess.

15. *Mobilize positive energizers who can motivate others.* They seek out positively energizing people to help uplift others around them. They marshal positive energizers to foster improvement and goal accomplishment. For example, they know individuals in their organization who positively energize others, and they mobilize them to help achieve needed outcomes and changes.

Not every positively energizing leader is characterized by all of these attributes, of course, and some attributes of de-energizers may not be entirely absent from positively energizing leaders. It is clear, however, that de-energizing behaviors diminish positive energy and reduce the effectiveness of leaders in relation to their employees. Most of these attributes are recognizable in individuals who are judged to be positively energizing, and, importantly, this list of attributes is not uncommon. None of the attributes is beyond the reach of most individuals. It is possible for almost anyone to develop these characteristics and, therefore, to develop attributes of positively energizing leadership.

The point is, positive energy can be developed and shared with everyone. And, most importantly, the research is clear: when leaders display these attributes, organizations flourish more than when the attributes are absent.

EMPIRICAL EVIDENCE

This last statement is verified by my own research on these attributes of positive energizers. A sample of 600 middle- and upper-management employees in organizations from a variety of industries (e.g., government, finance, construction, education, arts, and entertainment) was investigated. A version of the survey instrument is reproduced in resource 1. Respondents rated the leaders of their organizations on the 15 attributes of positively energizing leadership. They also provided organizational performance data on five dimensions: *productivity* (achieving targets and goals; accomplishing desired outcomes), *quality* (mistake- and error-free; on time or ahead of schedule), *employee morale* (satisfied, engaged employees; low turnover), *customer satisfaction* (loyal customers; few if any complaints), and *financial strength* (strong revenues; income exceeds expenditures).

The results showed that the higher the scores on the energizing attributes, the higher the organizations' performance scores in those five outcomes. (See resource 1.) In particular, especially strong predictive power was associated with the attributes numbered 11 through 15 in table 3.1. That is, positive leaders who *inspire and provide meaning*, who are *trusting and trustworthy*, who are *genuine and authentic*, who *expect very high performance standards*, and who *gather positive energizers that can motivate others* have the strongest impact on organizational effectiveness. All of the attributes of positively energizing leaders were found to be important and predictive, but these five were especially powerful predictors of organizational success. In addition, productivity, employee morale, and customer satisfaction outcomes were the most strongly affected by positively energizing leaders. Quality and financial strength of the organizations had slightly less strong associations, although the associations were statistically significant. Figure 3.1 provides a summary of these findings.

These findings highlight the fact that positively energizing leaders do not need to display superhuman attributes. They are individuals who simply display behaviors that we all admire: inspiring others, showing integrity, and being genuine. They expect us to be better. And they involve others in accomplishing desired outcomes. As a result, the organizations they lead perform significantly better than industry averages.

RELATIONSHIPS, VIRTUOUSNESS, AND ENERGY

The attributes associated with positive outcomes in organizations are also the attributes associated with positive relationships. Relationships are more uplifting and

FIGURE 3.1

The strongest associations between energizing attributes and organizational performance

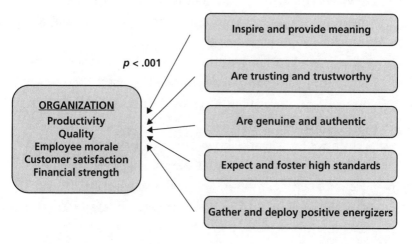

life-giving when these attributes are present compared with when they are not. It is also important to note that positive relationships can be relatively momentary (as in a brief interaction with a cashier, a receptionist, or a passerby on the street) or enduring interactions with someone with whom we work or live over time. Both short-term and long-term relationships matter, and even onetime, short-lived interactions can be positively energizing or energy depleting.

The characteristics of enriching, positive relationships have been addressed in a large array of scholarly and popular literature, and exceptionally excellent work has been conducted by my colleagues Jane Dutton,[2] Wayne Baker,[3] Gretchen Spreitzer,[4] and Jody Gittell[5] as well as by the Relational Coordination Network. In their work, these scholars focus on high-quality connections (momentary interactions), flourishing interactions, enduring associations, and relational coordination (the mutually reinforcing process of communicating and relating for the purpose of task accomplishment). The work of these scholars has had a major impact on understanding the literature on relational energy, and I encourage you to learn more about their work from the references at the end of the book.

In brief, this work shows that positive relationships are enablers of above-average outcomes physiologically, psychologically, emotionally, and organizationally. For example, evidence links the positive effects of social relationships with social phenomena such as career mobility,[6] mentoring and resource acquisition,[7] power,[8] and social capital.[9] Studies also show that positive social relationships have significant effects on longevity and recovery from illness.[10] That is, positive social relationships—the uplifting connections associated with individuals' interpersonal interactions—have beneficial effects on a variety of aspects of human behavior and health.

This chapter supplements the work of these colleagues by focusing on a set of attributes and behaviors that have received much less attention in leadership research. The primary intent of this discussion is to complement the literature regarding how to build and foster positively energizing relationships.

Figure 3.2 summarizes a set of behaviors that are especially important in producing positively energizing

FIGURE 3.2

Virtuousness, relationships, and positive energy

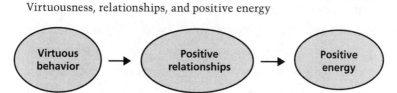

leadership but that have received sparse attention in the literature on leadership and organizational performance. Specifically, this discussion demonstrates that *virtuous behavior* is among the most important factors leading to *flourishing relationships*, which, in turn, lead to *positive energy*. Many of the attributes of positive energizers that emerged from our interviews in table 3.1, as it turns out, are consistent with what is often labeled as virtuous behavior.

VIRTUOUSNESS

The concept of virtuousness is rooted in the Latin word *virtus*, or the Greek *arête*, meaning "excellence." More recently, virtuousness has been described as representing the best of the human condition, the most ennobling behaviors and outcomes of people, the excellence and essence of humankind, and the highest aspirations of human beings.[11] Thomas Aquinas,[12] Aristotle,[13] and many other well-known philosophers proposed that virtuousness is rooted in human character and represents what human beings ought to be, humankind's inherent goodness, humanity's very best qualities, or being in complete harmony with the will of God. Virtuousness—the highest aspirations to which human beings aspire—is a commonly accepted standard in all cultures.[14] Whereas the nature of its demonstration may differ across cultures, virtuousness is universally agreed upon as good for all.[15] It serves as a stable, consensual standard, especially in times characterized by VUCA.

In functional terms, virtuousness is claimed to be evolutionarily developed because it allows people to live together, pursue collective ends, and protect against those who endanger the social order.[16] Thus, from a genetic or biological perspective, virtuousness plays a role in the development and perpetuation of humanity. This also explains why virtuousness is highly prized and admired, and why virtuous individuals are almost universally revered, emulated, and even sainted. They help perpetuate the human species.[17] Miller pointed out that a selective genetic bias for human moral virtuousness exists.[18] He argued that even mate selection evolved at least partly on the basis of displays of virtuousness.

This explains why virtuousness and the heliotropic effect are so closely connected. Virtuous actions are lifegiving and life-perpetuating, and this is the same definition associated with the heliotropic effect given in chapter 1. Human beings are inherently inclined toward that which gives or enables life, and, as it turns out, virtuousness is also heliotropic.

Several scholars have provided evidence that the human inclination toward virtuousness is inherent and evolutionarily developed.[19] Some have proposed, for example, that inherent virtuousness develops in the brain before the development of language.[20] Neurobiological studies show that individuals have a basic instinct toward morality and are organically inclined to be virtuous.[21] One study asserted that all human beings are "genetically disposed" to acts of virtuousness, and observing and experiencing virtuousness helps unlock the human predisposition toward behaving in ways that benefit others.[22]

Studies demonstrate, for example, that even before children are old enough to learn about civil behavior, they have inclinations toward fairness, generosity, and compassion. Infants as young as three months old exhibited behaviors indicative of moral virtue in experiments with puppets. When given a choice between a helpful, virtuous puppet and a puppet that did not help or that hindered another, children overwhelmingly preferred puppets that exhibited helpful, generous, and virtuous behavior.

Other studies confirm that children as young as 10 months old demonstrate virtuous behaviors (including generosity, altruism, fairness, and cooperation) when put in situations in which a choice was provided to them. The children in this study demonstrated inherent generosity, even more than that demonstrated by their more rational parents.[23]

Another study of 19-month-old children (the age at which children are most prone to exhibit temper tantrums and physical aggression when they do not get what they want) revealed that most children exhibited generosity even when they were disadvantaged by doing so. For example, a majority of children who had missed lunch and were especially hungry returned a fruit treat to another person who expressed a desire for it.[24]

Another set of studies has also demonstrated the benefits of virtuousness on heart rhythms and physiological coherence, which, in turn, predict longevity in life.[25] Heart rhythm oscillation is more stable and predictable when individuals are in a virtuous state. In addition, in an earlier book, *Positive Leadership,* I report a variety of positive physiological effects that are associated with virtuousness, such as wound healing, cortisol levels, experienced pain, and brain activation in ADHD children.[26]

ON THE OTHER HAND

Whereas virtuousness is heliotropic, common human experience as well as scientific evidence also support the idea that individuals have a strong reaction to negative experiences. One authoritative and comprehensive review from 2001 describes what we now call a human negativity bias. Baumeister and colleagues articulated the conclusion of their literature review with the article's title: "Bad Is Stronger Than Good."[27] Their review concluded that human beings react more strongly to negative phenomena than to positive phenomena or to stimuli that threaten their existence or signal maladaptation. Negative events have a greater impact than positive events of the same type (e.g., losing friends or money has a larger impact than winning friends or money; it takes longer for negative emotions to dissipate; less information is needed to confirm a negative trait in others; people spend more thought time on negative relationships than positive ones). This raises the question, How can virtuousness and positive energy be heliotropic if bad is stronger than good?

In three controlled experiments, Wang, Galinsky, and Murnighan found that a bias toward the negative has its strongest effects on emotions and psychological reactions, whereas reaction to the positive has its strongest effects on behavior. These authors concluded that "bad affects *evaluations* more than good does, but that good affects *behavior* more than bad does."[28] In other words, feelings are strongly affected when bad things happen, but behaviors are most strongly affected when good things happen. Negative energy makes us *feel* bad. Positive energy helps us take positive *action*.

A paradox exists in human experience, in other words.[29] Both positive inclinations and negative sensitivities exist simultaneously in human beings, and both are potential enablers of positive outcomes. Some of the greatest triumphs, most noble virtues, and highest achievements have resulted from the presence of the negative. Moreover, as people encounter danger, threats, and harm, their survival instincts lead them to pay attention to the negative. Bad takes precedence over good in the short run in order to survive, and negative energy gets more attention than positive energy. In such circumstances, people learn to minimize or ignore positive phenomena. In fact, they tend to negatively label anything positive as touchy-feely, soft, squishy, and irrelevant. They learn to ignore their natural heliotropic tendencies toward positive energy and toward virtuous behaviors.

One implication of this tendency to emphasize the negative in crisis situations is that conscious attention must be focused on positive relational energy and on virtuous behavior in order to overcome the powerful emotional effects of negative energy and threatening behavior. Negativity can become dominant, so virtuousness must be consciously pursued in order to produce life-giving, positive relational energy. Virtuousness lies at the core of the human experience (it is heliotropic), but it can easily be ignored in the presence of short-term crises.

CONCLUSION

The empirical evidence is strong that virtuousness is heliotropic in the sense that human beings are inherently inclined toward virtuous behavior; virtuous behavior is a key element in creating strong, flourishing relationships; and these relationships produce positive outcomes. An important point needs to be made, however, regarding this discussion of virtuousness.

Virtuousness, by definition, is inherently valued for its own sake. Virtuousness is not a means to obtain another more desirable end, but it is a valued end in itself. In fact, virtuousness in pursuit of another more attractive outcome ceases, by definition, to be virtuous. Gratitude, generosity, and integrity in search of recompense are not virtuous. If kindness toward employees is fostered in an organization, for example, solely to obtain a payback or an advantage, it ceases to be kindness and is, instead, manipulation. Virtuousness is associated with social betterment, but this betterment extends beyond mere self-interested benefit. Virtuousness creates social value that transcends the instrumental desires of the actor.[30] Virtuous actions produce an advantage to others in addition to, or even exclusive of, recognition, benefit, or advantage to the actor.[31]

Knowing the attributes of positively energizing leaders, and knowing that displaying virtuous behavior produces positive energy begs the questions: What can be done, specifically, to help develop positively energizing leadership? What actions can be taken? What training can be designed?

In the next chapter, I provide some specific ideas for developing positively energizing leadership. These suggestions are only a sampling of the possibilities for leadership development, of course, but they are behaviors that have proved useful in fostering virtuousness and positive relational energy.

4
DEVELOPING POSITIVELY ENERGIZING LEADERSHIP

The previous chapter established that virtuous behaviors are heliotropic, virtuousness is demonstrated even in early infancy, virtuousness produces positive relational energy, and virtuousness is associated with positive outcomes in organizations. The question remains: How might we help individuals become more effective positively energizing leaders by developing more virtuousness? What behaviors might we emphasize? This chapter highlights some virtuous behaviors that have not received much attention in the scholarly literature related to leadership and organizations. These are virtuous behaviors linked to both individual and organizational success even though, as pointed out in chapter 3, no additional benefit is needed for them to be of worth. Virtuousness is its own reward.

A great deal of emphasis in the scholarly and practical literature has been placed on helping employees feel valued, respected, and engaged at work. Countless blogs, seminars, consultant reports, and popular press articles emphasize the necessity of paying attention to employee needs. The assumption is that when people receive recognition, support, and encouragement, when their psychological and emotional requirements are met, when they feel secure in their jobs, and when their opinions are valued by their bosses, they will experience well-being and positive energy. Abundant evidence shows that when these conditions are met, absenteeism is low, productivity and profitability are high, and quality and safety improve.[1] Providing employees with what they desire is critical for successful performance.

Empirical evidence also confirms that the *contribution* that a person makes to others produces an even greater degree of positive relational energy. What people give to the relationship rather than what they receive from it is the more important factor in accounting for the positive effects of interactions. The demonstration of altruism, compassion, generosity, gratitude, integrity, and kindness, for example, has been found to be necessary for positive relationships to have their maximum positive impact on positive energy and performance.

THE VIRTUES OF GENEROSITY / ALTRUISM / CONTRIBUTION

In a study conducted by my colleague Jenny Crocker, college freshmen were asked to identify their goals for the school year. Goals were categorized as one of two types: achievement goals (e.g., getting high grades, being popular, getting elected to a club office) and contribution goals (e.g., making a difference, helping something improve). Most students claimed both types of goals, but different types of goals were dominant in different students. Participants were placed in two groups depending on which type of goal was dominant for them. The study followed these students for one year, measuring social factors (e.g., how well they got along with roommates, being elected to a club office), physical factors (e.g., how many minor physiological symptoms they experienced, such as the number of colds or illnesses, or days of class missed), and cognitive factors (e.g., grade point average, test scores on exams). At the end of the year, the investigation found that contribution goals, or the extent to which students focused on contributing to others, were significantly more predictive of success on each dimension (social, physiological, and cognitive outcomes) than achievement goals.[2]

A study of kidney dialysis patients corroborates the importance of contribution over receipt. In this investigation, kidney dialysis patients were measured on two factors: (1) the extent to which they were receiving love, support, and care from someone, and (2) the extent to which they were offering love, support, and concern to someone else. Even though the patients were physically constrained in their movements (they were attached to a dialysis machine), the second factor was found to be significantly more predictive of physical recovery and well-being than was the first factor. The higher the contribution score, the better off were the patients.[3]

Similar studies in multiple sclerosis patients showed the value of contribution for healing and positive health. In one study, half of the patient participants were assigned to receive a phone call each week in which another person expressed love, support, and concern to them. The other half of the patients were assigned to place a weekly phone call to someone in which they offered love, support, and concern to that person. At the end of the two-year period, patients were assessed on five factors: well-being, self-efficacy, physical activity, hope, and depression. An eightfold difference between the two groups was observed. Patients who *placed* the phone calls were eight times healthier on these five outcomes than were patients who *received* the phone calls.[4]

In still another study, older patients with high blood pressure were given $40 per week for three weeks. Half were instructed to spend the money on themselves, and the other half were instructed to spend the money on others (e.g., purchase a gift, donate to charity). Two years later, the patients who spent the money on others had significantly lower blood pressure than the patients who spent the money on themselves, and the effects matched the effects of antihypertensive medication or physical exercise as prescribed therapies.[5] In a similar study of older adults, those contributing to others' benefit had a 47 percent reduction in mortality risk.[6]

A study of individuals who had recently lost a spouse showed that those who provided instrumental support to others had no depression six months after their loss compared with substantial and lasting depression among those who merely received support but did not provide it. No receiving-support factors were positively correlated with an absence of depression, but giving-support factors were significantly correlated.[7] In an investigation of for-profit companies, employees who participated in programs in which they provided support to fellow employees, rather than receiving support, substantially increased their commitment to the organization as well as their inclination toward prosocial behaviors. Contributing rather than receiving was the key enabler.[8]

Sidebar 4.1 summarizes some of the empirically confirmed effects of generosity, altruism, and contribution. The point is that positive relational energy is more closely connected to these virtues than it is to receiving what we want or having our own needs satisfied. Both receiving and contributing are important in interpersonal interactions, of course, but it is what we do to help others flourish, rather than what we receive from others, that

Sidebar 4.1
Some Effects of Generosity, Altruism, and Contribution

- **Fosters positive relational energy**
- Improved social, cognitive, and physical performance
- Rated by others as more competent
- Improvement in personal well-being, physical activity, self-efficacy, hope, and depression
- Reduced blood pressure
- Improvement in mortality risk
- Avoidance of depression after significant loss
- Increased commitment to and engagement in employing organizations
- Inclined toward more prosocial behaviors

predicts our own well-being and positive energy. Positive relational energy is significantly enhanced when individuals express generosity and altruism and contribute to others' well-being.

THE VIRTUES OF GRATITUDE/RECOGNITION/HUMILITY

Another set of virtuous practices associated with positively energizing relationships relates to expressions of gratitude and recognizing the strengths and successes of others. According to a colleague, Bob Emmons (the world's foremost authority on the science of gratitude), expressions of gratitude also imply a sense of humility,[9] so these two virtues are combined into one category since they share a common attribute. Both virtues recognize and express appreciation for other people's strengths and contributions, and both avoid elevating oneself above others. Similar to the virtues of generosity, altruism, and contribution discussed above, the virtues of gratitude, recognition, and humility are also heliotropic. That is, human beings have a natural inclination toward displaying them.

A great deal of research has been conducted on the relationship between experiencing gratitude and resulting heart rhythms and heart health. For example, Bonnie and deWaal summarized a broad array of research studies on gratitude among both primates and young children.[10] They concluded that gratitude is inherent and has an evolutionary basis not only in humans but also in primates such as monkeys. Gratitude is universal, they discovered, across all cultures and peoples.

The association between gratitude and human health, well-being, and mortality has also been well established. For example, experiencing positive emotions such as gratitude and humility is associated with enhanced cognitive processing of sensory information,[11] highly ordered and coherent patterns in heart rhythms,[12] increased efficiency of fluid exchange, filtration, and absorption between the capillaries and tissues,[13] improved health and increased longevity,[14] cognitive flexibility and creativity,[15] and heart rate variability, which approaches the highest levels possible when these virtuous states are experienced. In one study of patients with Stage B heart failure, half were asked to keep a daily gratitude journal; after three months their hearts had healthier resting rates and showed significantly fewer biological signs that their heart disease was getting worse compared with those patients not keeping a gratitude journal.[16]

Several studies have been conducted in high school and college classrooms in which students were assigned to keep a journal during a semester. In these investigations, half the students were instructed to write down each day things for which they were grateful, or the best things that happened to them during the day. The other half wrote down events, interactions, or problems they encountered. At the end of the semester, students who kept gratitude journals experienced fewer physical symptoms such as headaches and colds; felt better about their lives as a whole; were more optimistic about the coming week; had higher states of alertness, attentiveness, determination, and energy; reported fewer hassles in their lives; engaged in more helping behavior toward other people; experienced better sleep quality; and had a sense of being more connected to others compared with the other students. In addition, they were absent and tardy less often and had higher grade point averages. Experiencing gratitude had a significant impact on student classroom performance as well as on their personal lives.[17]

In still another study of individuals entering psychotherapy for depression or anxiety, a group of patients were assigned to write a letter of gratitude to another person each week for three weeks. A second group of patients wrote about their deepest thoughts and impressions, and a third group did not write but just attended therapy sessions. Three months later, brain scans were conducted and a variety of well-being measures were collected. Regardless of gender, age, or initial levels of depression or anxiety, significant changes in positive neural activity were detected in the letter-writing group but not in the others. Areas of the brain most attuned to positive emotions, learning, and positive activity (the medial prefrontal cortex) were substantially affected compared with others. Despite the fact that only 23 percent of the patients actually sent the letters, the positive effects of the letters remained the same. Patients were advantaged just by writing the letter, not necessarily by having the recipient acknowledge receipt of the letter. Several months later, the positive effects of the gratitude intervention were found to be greater than the effects of the therapy itself.[18]

In organizational research, gratitude has been associated with improvements in productivity, quality of outputs, profitability, innovation, customer retention, and employee turnover.[19] Among organizations facing trying times and difficult challenges (such as downsizing or pandemic lockdowns), resilience and financial performance have also been shown to be significantly higher in organizations with high scores in demonstrating gratitude.[20]

Demonstrating leadership humility has been found to produce similar results. Humility is esteemed by all major religions and philosophies as a cardinal virtue, and the opposite of humility—hubris, arrogance, pride, narcissism—is universally condemned as undesirable. The generally accepted dimensions of leadership humility include the following:

- A demonstrated *willingness to view oneself accurately*—that is, to acknowledge mistakes, seek feedback, and express an openness to change as well as correctly recognize strengths and capabilities.
- A demonstrated *appreciation of others' strengths and weaknesses*—that is, to hold a positive view of others; to avoid competitive or comparative attitudes toward others; to avoid simplistic judgments of others such as competent/incompetent, stupid/intelligent, good/bad; to value the worth and contributions of others; and to express gratitude for others' contributions.

- *Teachability*, or an inclination to be open to feedback and learning—that is, to express a developmental readiness or thirst for learning and a willingness to ask for assistance.[21]

Not surprisingly, because these definitions share similar attributes (namely, recognizing and appreciating others), research emphasizing humility as a virtue produces outcomes similar to research on gratitude (although far more research has been conducted on the concept of gratitude). For example, leaders rated by their colleagues as being humble were found to produce higher levels of empowerment among employees as well as higher levels of engagement, commitment, and performance.[22] Leader humility, similar to gratitude, had a significant impact on positive interpersonal relationships, on team effectiveness, and on team learning, cohesion, and collective efficacy.[23] Sidebar 4.2 summarizes these various effects.

Studies of highly visible leaders who were identified as role models of humility (for example, Sam Walton, founder of Walmart; Mary Kay Ash, founder of Mary Kay Inc.; Herb Kelleher, founder of Southwest Airlines; Fred Smith, founder of Federal Express; and Ingvar Kamprad, founder of IKEA) have concluded that the success of their firms was highly dependent on the leadership humility demonstrated by each one. What they had in common was the capacity to build positive relational energy in their organizations.[24]

Sidebar 4.2

Some Effects of Gratitude, Recognition, and Humility

- **Fosters positive relational energy**
- Significant enhancement of heart rhythms and heart health
- Enhanced cognitive processing of information
- Increased efficiency of fluid exchange in the body
- Improved cognitive flexibility and creativity
- Improved academic performance in school
- Greater immunity to disease
- Higher levels of well-being, optimism, and sleep quality
- Less personal stress, depression, and anxiety
- Improved organizational performance related to profits, productivity, quality, innovation, customer satisfaction, and employee retention
- Enhanced team effectiveness, learning, cohesion, and collective efficacy

The empirical research confirms, in other words, that the virtues of gratitude, recognition, and humility are heliotropic—human beings have an inherent tendency toward them—and produce positive relational energy in both individuals and organizations.[25]

THE VIRTUES OF TRUST / INTEGRITY / HONESTY

A great deal of research has been conducted on the topic of trust, and excellent work has been produced by colleagues Rod Kramer[26] and Aneil and Karen Mishra.[27] It is almost universally accepted that without trust and integrity, nothing else works. Without trust, positively energizing leadership is impossible. When high levels of trust and integrity are present, however, a fertile foundation for positive energy is in place.

During the COVID-19 pandemic in 2020, Sweden's successful choice to avoid the comprehensive lockdowns instituted by many nations worldwide was attributed to having a "high trust" culture.[28] The country was described as a nation with high levels of trust in fellow citizens and in its institutions. In the United States, on the other hand, public trust was described as being quite low:

- Only 22 percent of citizens trust the media
- 8 percent trust political parties
- 15 percent trust the federal government
- 12 percent trust big companies
- 22 percent trust their employer
- 12 percent believe business executives have high ethical standards
- 12 percent believe that Congress has high ethical standards
- 34 percent think other people in general can be trusted.[29]

When high trust is not present, high levels of social control are required to ensure compliance and obedience. Most laws, most legislation, and most social control mechanisms (e.g., a requirement to show an ID card to vote or for entry, installed locks on most doors) exist primarily because we don't trust one another. It is obvious that societies operate much more efficiently when trust levels are high.

Similar to the virtuous behaviors discussed earlier, a natural inclination toward trust exists in human beings from the onset of life. Various scholars explain that emotional trust emerges from the sense of security that is experienced with a mother from the day the child is born.[30] This kind of trust in infancy emerges from being loved, cared for, and nurtured, and physiological development—including the functioning of internal organs, brain development, and sleep patterns—is enhanced. Human biological development, in other words, is closely related to the virtue of trust.[31]

Over time, trust becomes conditioned by the behaviors of others, so that honesty, fairness, and integrity come into play.[32] As individuals mature, trust becomes a critical feature in the development of positively energizing relationships. When trust, integrity, and honesty are present, a variety of positive benefits occur, as summarized in sidebar 4.3.

Empirical findings confirm that uncertainty and ambiguity are significantly reduced when trust is high, so complex situations can be managed more efficiently. Flexible work arrangements and teamwork become more feasible. Innovation and risk taking increase. Productivity improves as much as tenfold. Reciprocity among employees escalates. Expressions of gratitude are more frequent. Prosocial behavior and unselfish service accelerate. Generosity and sharing with others increase.

Sidebar 4.3

Some Effects of Trust, Integrity, and Honesty

- **Fosters positive relational energy**
- Enhanced development in infants
- Reduction in uncertainty
- Enhanced teamwork and flexible work arrangement
- Enhanced innovation and risk taking
- Dramatic improvement in productivity
- Increased reciprocity among employees
- Increases in prosocial behavior
- More display of generosity, altruism, and prosocial behavior
- Substantial reduction in inefficiency and waste

Cooperation improves.[33] Most importantly, the interpersonal relationships that provide positive energy are strengthened. Trusting relationships are almost always energizing, but positive energy is destroyed quickly when trust, honesty, and integrity deteriorate.

The key point being made thus far is that inclinations toward virtuousness are manifest from the time we are infants, and these inclinations are heliotropic. They also produce desirable outcomes in individuals and organizations. To repeat, however, the argument for virtuousness does not lie in the outcomes that such behaviors produce but in the inherent goodness and desirability they represent. We don't need to be virtuous to gain some other outcome or advantage. Virtuousness is its own reward. Yet, virtuous behaviors do indeed lead to positive energy, which suggests that virtuousness should be developed in every organization. In the next section, some of the ways these virtuous behaviors have been implemented in organizations are highlighted. (Also see resource 2 at the end of the book.)

APPLICATIONS OF GENEROSITY / ALTRUISM / CONTRIBUTION

The practices related to generosity, altruism, and contribution have been demonstrated in organizations in a variety of ways, and only a sampling of prescriptions is included here. These practices are among the most common and the most effective in enhancing and enabling positively energizing leadership.

• *Mentoring and Teaching.* In some organizations, when individuals demonstrate outstanding performance, they get a chance to mentor or coach someone else. Their reward is the opportunity to contribute. An example of one practice is to ask an employee to teach the group in the weekly staff meeting something new that he or she has recently learned. In the next meeting, another person is asked to do the same. After each person has had a chance to teach the group in a meeting, the process is repeated. On an ongoing basis, each employee not only learns something new but is given a chance to teach it to others.

• *One-Plus-One Awards.* The former head of faculty support in the Ross School of Business at the University of

Michigan provided an award to outstanding performers or those who achieved their goals. The application of this virtue occurred, however, when she also gave that individual a second award. The outstanding performer received two awards and could pass along the second award to someone else whom they wanted to recognize. Every time employees demonstrated outstanding performance, they received two awards and were able to recognize someone else.

• *Contribution Huddles.* A famous delicatessen in Ann Arbor, Michigan, holds weekly huddles with employees in which a list of items is written on a whiteboard. The items include such things as the number of dishes broken during the week, the total amount of tips, the time it took to go from sandwich order to delivery, and employee satisfaction ratings. Each person is responsible for reporting on a single item each week. The most important part of the report, however, is each person's plan to improve his or her single area of responsibility for the coming week. Each employee is given a chance to contribute one small but important improvement in the company each week.

• *Certificates.* Delta Airlines rewards frequent flyers in a special way. Upon obtaining a certain status level, frequent flyers are provided certificates they can present to a Delta employee for outstanding service. When a flight attendant, gate agent, or baggage handler exhibits outstanding performance, a passenger can award that employee a certificate. Teary eyes and a tendency to give hugs are not uncommon when Delta employees receive an award from a passenger. Delta recognizes its frequent flyers with a chance to contribute to someone else as a result of their loyalty.

• *Volunteering.* A number of organizations ask employees to volunteer time outside of work to benefit humanitarian organizations, schools, or not-for-profit groups. Some provide a certain percentage of paid time off for volunteering. In one organization, the CEO designated one particular day as Volunteer Day and closed the entire organization. He announced that employees could volunteer to assist in community service agencies or just stay home. To his surprise, 88 percent of his employees showed up to volunteer. The next year the employees asked when Volunteer Day would be scheduled, but the CEO replied that it was very expensive to shut down the company so he had not planned on a repeat. The employees insisted that this opportunity not be abandoned, so Volunteer Day now occurs on an annual basis.

• *The Best Thing You Did.* An acquaintance who is a senior executive has a small daughter who hated to go to school. This child would hang on to her mother's leg when it was time to go to school and would cry when her mother dropped her off, making the mother feel terrible. The girl's teacher suggested that the mother ask the child to report on the best thing that happened during the day as a way to help her focus on something positive. Asking that question each day after school improved the situation somewhat, but it was still difficult. The mother decided to change the question to "What is the best thing that you did for someone today?" Somehow, that made the difference. The child was excited each day to report on what she had done for someone else during the day at school.

The payoff, her mother reported, occurred when they took a trip to Disney World. They visited a restroom where a cleaning lady was present. Often, these service personnel are ignored or treated as just being in the way. This child went up to the cleaning lady and said, "I hope you have a magical day today." The woman began to cry. She replied, "I have worked here for 14 years and no one has ever wished for me to have a magical day." That incident, the mother reported, was the payoff—her daughter was consistently looking for ways to foster positive relational energy by making a small contribution every day.

APPLICATIONS OF GRATITUDE / RECOGNITION / HUMILITY

A variety of organizations with which I am familiar have also put into place practices that capitalize on the virtues of gratitude, recognition, and humility. Here are a few examples.

• *Gratitude Journals.* Several organizations, even those with thousands of employees, have given each employee a journal or a notebook and labeled it a "gratitude journal." All employees are asked to keep a journal in which, each day or at least each week, they record answers to one or more of these questions: What are you grateful for today? What is the best thing that has happened today? What would you miss if it were taken away? What are the small blessings for which you are most grateful?

• *Gratitude Walls.* In a variety of organizations, bulletin boards, whiteboards, or even glass walls or windows are given the title of "gratitude wall." In one case, an executive wrote with erasable marker the words "gratitude wall" on the outside of her glass office wall. That's all. Within an hour, an employee had written something for which she was grateful. Within the week, several other glass walls in the building had been given the same title and were filled with employee comments. Some organizations have created walls on which are attached envelopes with the name of each member of the organization. Stacks of blank cards are made available, and employees can write a note to any person they choose. They simply put the note into that person's envelope. This practice is also done in conferences and seminar locations where each attendee has an assigned envelope.

• *Gratitude Cards or Letters.* A senior executive in a large multinational firm (LG in Korea) asked his assistant to place five cards on his desk each day. "Thank you" was printed on one side of the card, and the other side was blank. He assigned himself the responsibility to write five gratitude or recognition notes to five different employees each day. He reported that this activity changed the climate of his entire top management team from a negative problem-focused orientation to a positive opportunity-based orientation.

Another executive wrote just one gratitude note to an employee each day. Seventeen years later, upon his retirement, the number of notes still in existence (those that were framed, on an office bulletin board, under the glass on a desk) numbered in the thousands. That was his primary legacy. Another executive made certain to write one letter each year to each employee's family expressing how important the employee is to the company and recognizing the major accomplishments of the year.

• *Positively Embarrass Someone.* In one large multinational firm that was facing a difficult financial situation, the CEO assigned each employee to positively embarrass another employee at least once per day. This meant that each person would compliment someone in front of someone else who cares. The intent was to focus on what was going well, what should be celebrated, and who should be thanked or congratulated. A few employees expressed discomfort at the assignment and initially thought that it was silly, superficial, or uncomfortable. It didn't take long, however, to have this one practice create a substantial impact on the company's culture, and resistance evaporated.

• *Begin Meetings.* Many organizations begin each department meeting or staff meeting by giving each attendee 60 seconds to share the best thing that has happened this past week, or to identify what should be celebrated. Even in large gatherings such as seminars or all-hands meetings, the first few minutes are taken to have each person turn to someone else in the crowd and share good news, gratitude, or celebrations. Every meeting begins with a burst of positive energy.

• *Availability and Openness.* The leaders of some of the highest-performing organizations I know demonstrate humility and openness by providing regular opportunities for employees to ask questions, offer suggestions, and influence decision making, even regarding important issues such as determining the future direction, values, and culture of the company. These opportunities are facilitated through town hall meetings, regular breakfasts between senior leaders and groups of employees, visits by leaders to employee offices, off-site events that involve employees' families in ongoing improvement initiatives, and regular opportunities for personal or leadership development through seminars, lunch-and-learn events, or stretch assignments. Leaders try hard to remain visible, available, and open to personal feedback and suggestions for improvement.

APPLICATIONS OF TRUST / INTEGRITY / HONESTY

• *Integrity.* Almost all leaders and organizations espouse honesty, but the ones that develop a reputation for trust and integrity share messages that are sometimes risky to share. They tell the truth, talk straight, and avoid spinning messages that they know could harm them if distorted or misunderstood. This may entail information about firm finances, mistakes, or external threats. Achieving high levels of trust is a product of having employees believe that they are not being deceived, that they are being counted on to help solve problems, and that they are relied on to make contributions.

• *Consistency.* In times of abundance, almost all organizations are able to live in harmony with espoused values—"People are our most important asset." "Customers come first." "Integrity is our most important value." "Quality is job one." In trying times, however, when budgets must be cut, the pressure is on to make dramatic changes, and espoused values are often put on the shelf as a way to cope with the crisis. Draconian and seemingly irrational actions are not infrequently implemented. The high-trust organizations remain consistent, do what they espouse, and are dependable. The environmental conditions do not determine their level of integrity. One example is the CEO of a major airline who refused to lay off employees during a major financial crisis. As the CEO put it:

> We could have furloughed at various times and been more profitable, but I always thought that was short-sighted. You want to show your people that you value them, and you're not going to hurt them just to get a little more money in the short term. Not furloughing people breeds loyalty. It breeds a sense of security. It breeds a sense of trust.[34]

• *Sacrifice.* The highest levels of trust are associated with a person's sacrificing something for the benefit of someone else. When it would be easy or desirable to make a decision or to take an action, but that desire is sacrificed in order to support or provide assistance to another, trust is almost automatic. By putting another person's welfare above one's own and demonstrating it, high-trust relationships (and positive relational energy) always result.

• *Competence.* Trust depends on the assumption that the necessary competence exists to obtain the desired outcome. That's why driver's license exams are given and why certifications are required of health-care professionals. In organizations, demonstrating competence is also a key to trust. Organizations in which employees feel empowered, where engagement is high, and where people feel valued are organizations in which individuals produce promised results, display competence, and show that they can perform at an especially high level. Demonstrated competence and trust go hand in hand.

• *Emotional Bank Account.* Many years ago a friend and former colleague, Stephen Covey, introduced the concept of the "emotional bank account."[35] This concept explains the extent to which a relationship is flourishing and energizing or is depleting and de-energizing. In positively energizing relationships, people make regular and consistent emotional deposits, even when it is inconvenient, and deposits are always greater than withdrawals. Deposits include things such as listening intently, acting with kindness, clarifying expectations, keeping commitments, not waiting to be asked, apologizing, being present, expressing gratitude, and smiling. The 15 behaviors in table 3.1 in chapter 3 are examples of deposits.

Withdrawals include things such as making insensitive statements, violating expectations, being discourteous, criticizing, interrupting, ignoring, or being sarcastic. These are behaviors represented by the right-hand column in table 3.1 in chapter 3. Trust and positive relational energy in a relationship are dependent on making more deposits than withdrawals. I know of organizations where leaders consciously keep track of the balance of their emotional bank account with their employees. They know that they will occasionally need to make a withdrawal, and they want to make sure that enough deposits have been made so that sufficient positive relational energy is available.

WHAT ABOUT BLACK HOLES?

Quite frequently, I have been asked by executives or employees how to deal with individuals in their organizations who are characterized as "black holes." These are negative, divisive, solemn, caustic, and abrasive people. They suck the energy out of everyone with whom they interact. They are the reverse of positive energizers.

The comment often made by these questioners goes something like this: It's fine to develop and encourage positive energizers, but I have folks in my organization who are the opposite. They wrench the vitality out of everyone else and diminish positive relational energy.

The trouble is, it does not take many black holes to destroy any positive energy that might exist. How can I effectively respond to this kind of person?

My experience, not based on empirical evidence, is that in such circumstances, a four-stage process might be considered. The goal is to act consistently with positively energizing principles but still solve the problem of black-hole behavior.

Stage 1 is to ask questions in an attempt to understand the individual's situation, perspective, or concerns. Then, after seeking to understand, use supportive communication principles to provide descriptive feedback.[36] The goal of supportive communication is to provide corrective or negative feedback in a way that builds and strengthens the relationship rather than creates defensiveness (a sense of being attacked) or disconfirmation (a sense of feeling worthless).

This kind of feedback uses three steps. First, describe the behavior that occurred or that you think needs to be modified. As objectively and dispassionately as possible, talk about the behavior instead of about the person himself or herself. Identify elements of the behavior that can be confirmed by someone else. Identify accepted standards rather than relying merely on personal opinion or preferences. Avoid evaluative statements such as "You are wrong" or "You have a problem" or "You don't understand."

Second, describe your (or others') reactions to the behavior, or describe the consequences that have resulted. Identify the deleterious effects that have occurred. Rather than projecting onto another person the cause of the problem, focus instead on the reactions or consequences the behavior has produced.

Third, suggest a more acceptable alternative. This focuses the discussion on a suggested alternative, not on the person's self-worth. It also helps the other person save face and avoid feeling personally criticized or denigrated. The esteem you hold for the person is separated from the behavior. Self-esteem is preserved because it is the behavior (something controllable), not the person, that can be modified. Most people will respond favorably to feedback that is authentic, helpful, and kind and is designed to help them flourish. This is especially the case when suggestions of more acceptable behavior are offered.

If stage 1 doesn't work, or if the person remains defensive or recalcitrant, a second stage can be applied. Stage 2 involves offering coaching, training, or growth opportunities. Developing an improvement plan is often helpful because offenders frequently say something like, "Well, this is just the way I am." "I don't know any other way to behave." "This is just my style."

When the motive toward the offending person is to help him or her flourish, providing more acceptable alternatives may be a special favor. Coaching sessions may be designed in which the objective is to help individuals behave in ways that add value rather than detract from value, help other people rather than diminish other people, and create positive energy rather than deplete positive energy. Almost everyone will respond favorably to genuine attempts by someone to help them improve in specific ways.

In some circumstances, however, individuals may still remain obstinate black holes, so a third stage may be appropriate. Stage 3 involves making the person peripheral. It is not unusual to encounter instances where the black holes are specialists who are indispensable to the organization, individuals who account for substantial amounts of the organization's success, or people with vitally important talents. Stage 3 suggests that, figuratively speaking, the microphone is taken out of their hands, their opportunities for interaction are markedly reduced, and the negative virus is isolated. Positively energizing leaders help these people do their work, but as much as possible, they are kept from infecting the rest of the system. The motive is, again, to help this person succeed in his or her role but without incurring more cost than benefit to the organization.

In rare instances, stage 4 becomes necessary when the energy-killing problem remains despite genuine and empathetic efforts to make things better. The prescription for such a scenario is to help the person flourish elsewhere. This does not mean summarily dismissing the person or getting rid of him or her out of exasperation. Rather, it means that leaders communicate the message: You are not flourishing in this environment, and the rest of us are not flourishing. Let's find a place where you can flourish, but it will not be here.

The welfare of the person is never abandoned, and positively energizing leadership is never discontinued.

Instead, the motive remains to help the individual fulfill his or her potential. Note, however, that this is stage 4, not stage 1. A great deal of investment has occurred before the person is ushered out.

Often when we encounter black holes, we ignore them, fight with them, or just eliminate them. Positively energizing leaders maintain a virtuous approach toward individuals, even when it is difficult or uncomfortable.

CONCLUSION

It needs to be repeated that virtuousness is heliotropic in that, from infancy, human beings are inherently inclined toward virtuous practices. They thrive physiologically as well as socially when virtuousness is present. It is also the case that, by definition, virtuousness is inherently valued for its own sake. It is not a means to obtain another end, but it is a valued end in itself.

Nonetheless, the evidence is clear that virtuousness is unequivocally associated with social betterment, improved organizational performance, and, most importantly, the creation of positively energizing relationships. This chapter advocates the demonstration of virtuous behaviors not only because they lead to positive outcomes but also because they lead to the only kind of energy that does not deplete with use and does not require recovery time. Virtuousness lies at the heart of positively energizing leadership.

Three clusters of virtuous practices, which are associated with positively energizing leadership, have been highlighted, and a few examples of practical applications of these virtues have been described. The intent is to help leaders identify practices that bring about small, easily implemented steps that can produce positive relational energy.

The next chapter offers examples of the use of positively energizing leadership in major organizational change initiatives. In each instance, the organization found itself in extraordinarily difficult circumstances, and it was the demonstration of positively energizing leadership that led to dramatic success. In each case, the kind of organization being described represents an unusual setting for positive change initiatives. Each is a loosely coupled system without a single leader that could mandate change. Positive relational energy was the key to success.

5
EXAMPLES OF POSITIVELY ENERGIZING LEADERSHIP

This chapter highlights four examples of positively energizing leadership and its impact on organizational performance. In each case the positive energy displayed by the leadership team was not the only factor that produced outstanding results, but it was certainly a key element in accounting for performance that, in some cases, far exceeded expectations. In each example, the leader of the organization did not have the power or authority to mandate a desired change or strategy himself or herself. Positively energizing leadership was among the only resources available.

The cases are Laureate, Saudi Telecom, the Business and Finance Division at the University of Michigan, and Tecmilenio University. These examples were chosen because they represent diverse types of organizations facing very different circumstances, but each was influenced by positively energizing leadership that exemplified the positive attributes enumerated in the previous chapters.[1]

LAUREATE

An example of the impact of positive energy at the top of an organization occurred in the world's largest university consortium, Laureate (which, in 2017, owned 69 universities in 12 regions throughout the world). At the time, Laureate had more than 1 million students and approximately 135,000 staff members. These institutions of higher education are located in Central and South America, Australia, New Zealand, Europe, India, and Africa, and several are considered to be the most prestigious in their respective nations.

The CEO and the president of Laureate (respectively, Eilif Serck-Hanssen and Ricardo Berckemeyer) determined that positive leadership would become the core principle on which innovation and culture change would be based in the future. These two leaders had previously been exposed to positive leadership principles through association with Jim Mallozzi, highlighted in the introduction to this book. They were aware that Laureate was facing significant financial pressures as well as senior executive turnover. It was clear that the status quo was not a viable strategy for future success.

Senior leaders in this worldwide organization—including presidents, chancellors, and chief academic officers of the various universities throughout the world—were brought together for a three-day intensive workshop. The workshop centered on reviewing the empirical research that established the credibility of positive leadership and, in particular, illustrated the power of positive energy in accounting for institutional improvement. In addition, examples of practices that fostered positive energy were reviewed.

As part of this workshop, participants identified "positive energizers" in each of the 12 geographic regions of the world in which Laureate operated. Positive energizers were defined, in this instance, as individuals who convey enthusiasm, engender positive relationships, help other people flourish, and can be relied on to uplift and elevate the climate of their units. Attributes discussed in table 3.1 of chapter 3 in this volume were shared, and together, these senior executives identified a group of 46 individuals they deemed to be positive energizers.

These energizers were brought together for a three-day intensive workshop on positive leadership and given a 90-in-90 Challenge. The challenge was to *infect* 90 percent of all Laureate staff members throughout the world with positive energy in 90 days. To be infected meant that individuals could teach or explain to others what positively energizing leadership is, and they would have attempted a 1 percent improvement aimed at demonstrating positive leadership.

No centrally prescribed agenda was mandated for how the 90-in-90 Challenge was to be approached, and energizers were free to address the task in whatever ways they felt appropriate. Among the activities implemented by these various groups are those listed in resource 2 at the end of the book.

In 90 days, 93.3 percent of the 135,000 staff members had been infected, and more than 120,000 hours of

FIGURE 5.1

Scores on eight dimensions of positive practices

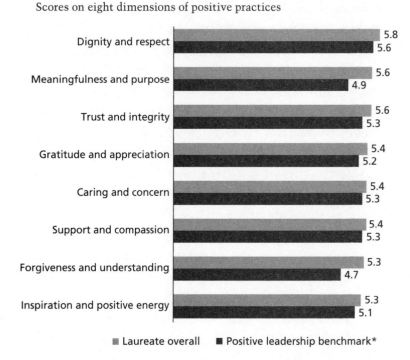

■ Laureate overall   ■ Positive leadership benchmark*

training and workshops had been conducted. Forums, seminars, celebrations, task forces, classroom instruction, coaching, physical symbols, and theatrical productions were developed to accomplish the task. In follow-up surveys conducted after the events, 95 percent of participants indicated that they would recommend this training to others, and 98 percent indicated that they gained new knowledge on how they could enhance their institution's performance. Figure 5.1 shows the results of a worldwide survey of employees after the 90-in-90 Challenge. On each dimension, scores improved over the three-month period.

An important part of the initiative's success was the personal examples set by Serck-Hanssen and Berckemeyer. They made their calendars publicly available so they could be held accountable for the amount of time they dedicated to the positive leadership initiative. They wrote gratitude notes to employees each week. The incentive and recognition systems were updated to reflect positive energy principles. They were clearly demonstrating attributes of positively energizing leaders mentioned in chapter 3 such as sharing plum assignments, role-modeling problem solving, focusing on opportunities as much as the obstacles, clarifying meaningfulness, and utilizing a large number of positive energizers throughout the world. Positively energizing leadership from the top was unequivocally part of the formula for success.

In addition to the overall institutional strategies that were implemented worldwide, 14 different experiments were conducted to assess the impact of positive practices and positive energy on students in classrooms. In several Laureate universities across three continents, instructors in different disciplines were invited to participate in an investigation of positive practices in the classroom. Fourteen faculty members volunteered to participate in the study.[2] These instructors agreed to implement a variety of positive practices in their classrooms and to model positive energy—again, with no prescribed curriculum or approach. The disciplines in the study included accounting, analytic design methods, architecture, art, economics, education, human resources, nutrition, physiology, and statistics.

FIGURE 5.2

Effects of positive leadership classes on students at universities in India and Spain

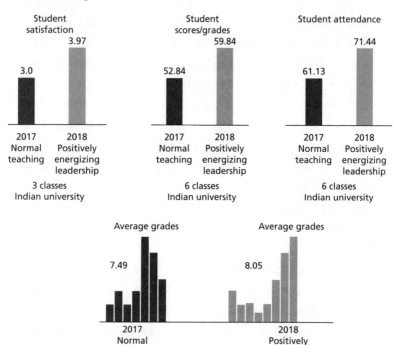

Instructors were exposed to principles of positive energizing and positive leadership in a workshop. They were then asked to incorporate whatever practices they desired in their classrooms. Data were collected comparing the positive leadership classes with the classes taught by the same instructors the year before. Figure 5.2 provides the comparisons.

Compared with the courses taught by the same instructors the year before implementing positive practices in their classrooms, three classes in a university in
India (upper-left chart in figure 5.2) showed student satisfaction scores almost a full point higher on a 1–5 scale.
In another analysis of six different classrooms at the
same university (upper-middle chart), average student
test scores and grades were 7 percentage points higher,
and student attendance (upper-right chart) was 10 percentage points higher. In four separate classrooms in a
Spanish university (lower chart), average student test
scores and course grades were a half point higher on a
10-point scale after exposing students to positive leadership and positive energy.

These were not rigorously controlled experiments, of
course, and clearly a variety of other factors could have
been at play in accounting for the results. The outcomes
do suggest, however (as did the Laureate senior executives in follow-up interviews), that positively energizing
practices had a nontrivial impact on the institutions and
on students in the classroom, even across different academic disciplines and national cultures.

SAUDI TELECOM

A second example of the impact of positively energizing
leadership comes from the Kingdom of Saudi Arabia, an
absolute monarchy ruled by the royal family of Al Saud.
It has become clear that the oil resources that drive the
country's economy will eventually run out and that the

carbon-based economy on which the country relies (mainly oil and gas revenues) will need to be supplanted by a digitally based economy. The approach that Saudi Arabia took to begin this transformation was to privatize a government ministry, change it into a nimble, forward-looking, for-profit business, and then use this transformation as the exemplar for the nation's economic and cultural modernization.

The government ministry selected to be privatized was Saudi Telecom (STC), the telecommunications provider for the kingdom. Its successful transformation, as it turned out, depended to a large degree on the positively energizing leadership of Khaled H. Biyari, who was appointed CEO in 2015.

Within five years, STC became the leading national provider of telecommunication services in the Gulf region and was operating 11 subsidiaries in eight countries. Market capitalization doubled while competitors' market cap decreased by about 50 percent. Brand value grew from $2.8 billion to $6.2 billion, and STC is now one of the top three brands in the Middle East. STC's High Potential Development Program was awarded "Best Talent Program in the Gulf" by the Arabian Society for Human Resource Management in 2018. Scores on McKinsey Consulting firm's organizational health indicator were initially among the lowest in the world in 2013, but they soared from 33 on a 100-point scale to 71, the largest five-year increase in McKinsey's database.

How did Biyari lead such a dramatically successful transformation in STC? His positively energizing leadership was universally lauded by employees as the key to STC's success.[3] In particular, Biyari's leadership was characterized by three key attributes associated with positive relational energy: helping others flourish through fostering personal growth, recognizing and expressing appreciation for others' contributions, and demonstrating openness to feedback for self-improvement (attributes also characteristic of leadership humility).

Helping others flourish. As just one example of this positively energizing initiative, Biyari instituted the role of "health doctor" in each of STC's units and assigned one health doctor to each senior leader. These individuals were not medical doctors looking after physical health; rather, health doctors were charged with helping to improve organizational health and leadership effectiveness. Their role was to provide each senior executive with ideas for how to be a more positively energizing leader. Corporate funding was provided for health doctors to implement ideas and identify needed changes, and they were given total freedom to make suggestions and initiate improvements.

Biyari commented, "We are trying to change leaders into listeners." One health doctor—a volunteer who, in each unit, supplemented his or her normal job responsibilities with the health doctor role—was assigned to shadow each general manager or vice president. Each of these senior leaders received ongoing suggestions for personal development and for organizational advancement.

Appreciating others' contributions. Instead of developing and disseminating a vision statement and list of corporate values from the office of the CEO, Biyari held multiple workshops throughout the firm in which he asked employees: Who do we want STC to be? What are the values that we want to characterize our company? What is the best company we can imagine? From these workshops, 57 values emerged from employees. Employees in STC had never before been given the opportunity to help craft the ideal organization and its future, but holding these workshops provided a different kind of message from Biyari: "Our best intangible asset is people engaging and caring for one another."

Biyari's team reduced the list of 57 values to the following five core themes:

- *Customer first*: "We serve our customers passionately—external and internal."
- *Innovation*: "We capture the new and deliver it to our markets."
- *Lead with agility*: "I am an agile leader who performs in a changing world."
- *Build trust*: "I say what I think, do what I say, and do it well."
- *One STC*: "We collaborate to deliver STC's vision."

Biyari himself then supplemented this list of values with an additional one. From his perspective, the list omitted a direct focus on employees, so he superimposed the value "Employees First" as the foundation on which all others values rested. Biyari reported that in practical terms, this meant changing human resources from "guardians of the firm" to "we care about you" representatives. He created a weekly CEO blog emphasizing and highlighting the variety of Employees First initiatives being implemented.

These initiatives took a variety of forms. For example, coffee, tea, and water were free for employees rather than having employees pay for their own. All furniture, working spaces, and bathrooms were remodeled and upgraded, and employees' workspaces became modern, clean, and comfortable and had positive themes. Attractive common spaces were developed that included decompression locations with games, puzzles, books, and comfortable seating where employees could relax and get off-line for a period of time.

Importantly, Biyari created a learning academy, the STC Academy, dedicated to developing world-class leadership and helping to develop the positive culture change initiatives. All leaders within STC attended workshops and development sessions taught by university faculty members from throughout the world. The quality and effectiveness of the training were so high that, even when given a choice to attend training from the world's best universities, STC employees selected the STC Academy as their preferred source.

Openness to feedback. Biyari's fundamental approach to positively energizing leadership was captured by his statement "If you can touch people's hearts, and help them believe by listening to them, they do incredible things." Biyari instituted regular visits to employees' and customers' offices, a first for STC. This led other vice presidents and general managers to do the same, so that the norm at STC is now for senior leaders to conduct regular visits to subordinates' work spaces to encourage feedback. The guiding question asked by these senior leaders during their visits is "What would you like your leaders to do better?"

Biyari also made the decision early in his tenure to attract female employees. Traditionally, men and women did not work together in Saudi Arabia; in 2016, fewer than 10 of STC's 17,000 total employees were women. To attract more women, Biyari directed the construction of a separate building available only to women so that they would feel safe and comfortable at work. By 2018, more than 300 women were employed at STC, and that number has continued to grow. Female employees were given a voice in company policy and strategy, and a female-only building is no longer needed.

Of course, not every decision and action taken by Biyari was accepted without controversy or resistance. The cultural norms in Saudi Arabia still have a great deal of influence over the way organizations operate. Biyari's leadership was extraordinary, however, in challenging the traditional patterns of leadership typical of a Saudi governmental culture. He demonstrated that positively energizing leadership, including expressing humility, getting personal, trusting others, and being genuine and authentic, can, indeed, be successful across multiple countries and cultures.

BUSINESS AND FINANCE DIVISION
AT THE UNIVERSITY OF MICHIGAN

The Business and Finance Division (B&F) at the University of Michigan consists of approximately 2,700 employees in six diverse areas: facilities and operations (e.g., custodial, grounds keeping, bus drivers), finance (e.g., auditing, budgeting), investments (e.g., portfolio management, endowment), information (e.g., data management, analytics), human resources (e.g., benefits, counseling), and shared services (e.g., computer systems, payroll). Forty-five different organizations report to the head of the division. Managing such a diverse and loosely coupled entity presented a major challenge. The division served as a hub for complaints and dissatisfaction in the university.

The head of B&F also served as the executive vice president as well as the chief financial officer of the university. A new leader, Kevin Hegarty, was hired from outside the university to lead the division, and soon thereafter, he embarked on a culture change initiative focused on creating a positive organization. The intent was to help staff members at all levels believe that what they do matters, and that they can make a positive difference.

One major initiative in which Hegarty engaged was to bring together the leadership group of approximately 175 leaders in the top four levels of B&F. He shared with this group positive leadership principles and the concept of positive energy. The group agreed to collectively encourage the entire division to implement a 90-in-90 Challenge. The challenge involved identifying a group of

160 positive energizers across the B&F division and charging them with the task of infecting 90 percent of the division's employees with positive practices in 90 days. In this case, infecting meant to expose 90 percent of B&F staff to the principles of positive leadership and engage them in at least one related positive exercise within 90 days. In addition, staff members are invited to join the 1 percent positive change club by personally committing to one positive practice.

Senior leaders and the volunteer positive energizer group engaged in daylong forums and workshops to learn about positive leadership and positive energy and to begin to plan their interventions. No specific activities were prescribed, and individual departments created their own strategies to accomplish the challenge. A sampling of the activities that occurred during the 90-day period are listed in resource 2 at the end of the book.

A central website was established for sharing ideas and asking for help, as well as a site where energizers could download resources, templates, and other materials. Positive energizers were encouraged to share highlights of what was going well—a.k.a. bright spots—via a central email location. Four main areas of activity were targeted: building positive relationships, creating purpose and meaning, focusing on strengths, and fostering positive communications.[4]

In a survey of the positive energizers at the outset of the challenge, 96 percent expressed confidence in being able to apply positive practices, and 94 percent were already trying new positive initiatives with their departments. After the completion of the 90-in-90 Challenge, not only did B&F exceed the 90 percent goal for infecting employees, but dozens of unique and innovative activities were implemented as part of the challenge. The year before the intervention, about 500 unique initiatives had been attempted throughout B&F. The year after the intervention, the number had increased to more than 1,400 initiatives. (See resource 2 for a list of some of the initiatives implemented in the 90-in-90 Challenge.) Moreover, an employee opinion survey indicated a substantial improvement in the organization's climate compared with the results from two years earlier (see figure 5.3).

FIGURE 5.3

Improvements in employee opinion scores as a result of the positive culture initiative

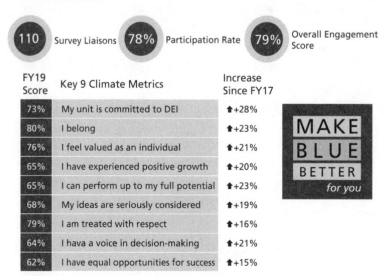

FY19 Score	Key 9 Climate Metrics	Increase Since FY17
73%	My unit is committed to DEI	⬆+28%
80%	I belong	⬆+23%
76%	I feel valued as an individual	⬆+21%
65%	I have experienced positive growth	⬆+20%
65%	I can perform up to my full potential	⬆+23%
68%	My ideas are seriously considered	⬆+19%
79%	I am treated with respect	⬆+16%
64%	I hava a voice in decision-making	⬆+21%
62%	I have equal opportunities for success	⬆+15%

Source: Used with permission of Kevin Hegarty, EVP-CFO, University of Michigan.

Even in this loosely coupled system with employees ranging from bus drivers to pipefitters serving in campus tunnels to counselors for addiction problems to individuals managing millions of dollars in financial investments, the intervention that focused on positive practices appeared to knit the unit together and achieve results that had not been experienced before. Hegarty's message to the division upon completion of the 90-in-90 Challenge illustrates his positively energizing approach:

I wanted to send a note to congratulate you on completing the 90/90 Challenge. Even with everything that has happened in the last three months, you continued to support your colleagues, build community and create positive emotions by promoting gratitude, kindness and fun. We could never have imagined we would face a global pandemic in the midst of this initiative, but words cannot express how grateful I am that you were serving in these important roles—our B&F staff needed your positive energy more than ever! Thank you!!

I know each of you had to shift your original plans and reimagine your efforts to accommodate teams working remotely, working in rotations, or working on campus while social distancing. And while it was not an easy pivot, you did so remarkably well. We are still receiving final reports, but the numbers are looking terrific. The teams that have reported so far have reached an average of 90% of staff in their areas, with many reaching 100%—Wow!

We are so lucky that so many of you are planning to continue in your roles as positive energizers, to continue to encourage your colleagues to make a 1% positive change, and to continue to support our goals to create a positive and inclusive workplace for everyone.

Our organization, and the people within it, are better off because of you. I want to invite you to take a minute and reflect on everything you've accomplished. I am absolutely amazed by the creativity and ingenuity you've brought to your roles—you can see many, many examples on our website. Thank you for everything you have done, and continue to do, to make our organization, and our world, a more positive place.[5]

TECMILENIO UNIVERSITY

Tecmilenio University in Monterrey, Mexico, was established to help make higher education, especially technical education, available to a broader portion of the Mexican population. Between its founding in 2002 and the year 2010, Tecmilenio gradually increased enrollments to about 3,000 students. After these first few years of successful operation, however, Tecmilenio's enrollment began to decline. In 2010, for example, enrollment totaled 3,120 students; in 2011, enrollment was 2,991 students (–4%); and in 2012, enrollment had fallen to 2,844 students (–5%). The university had developed a reputation as being a low-cost, second-class institution, and annual staff turnover averaged almost 100 percent. Student retention was only 40 percent.

The president of Tecmilenio, Hector Escamilla, determined that to turn the institution around would require a dramatically different strategy than had been pursued in the past. He hired several key staff members to help him develop and achieve this new strategy. Between 2012 and 2016, the Tecmilenio staff aggressively sought exposure to positive psychology and positive organizational scholarship[6] to create a foundation for a complete transformation of the university. Hector attended conferences around the world to become well versed in positive leadership.

This exposure led Hector to develop a new model for the university where students, staff, faculty, and alumni would pursue personal and institutional well-being and happiness as the primary outcomes of their higher education experience. Tecmilenio's formal mission was stated as "We prepare people to flourish, have a purpose in life, and prepare the skills that can help them achieve their purpose in order to benefit society."

This new university vision—to create the world's first well-being and happiness university—was based on three primary characteristics: (1) a customized education experience where students could choose up to 40 percent of their coursework (which provided substantial flexibility to pursue marketable competencies); (2) a learning-by-doing approach supported by a competency-based education model, co-op semester, laboratories, faculty members from industry, and industry advisory boards for the campus; and (3) providing practical tools that produce well-being, life satisfaction, and happiness in the entire Tecmilenio University as well as the Monterrey, Mexico, community. The goal was to reflect positive principles in all facilities, messages, products, services, rituals, and behaviors associated with the institution.

Hector organized 12 teams that included representatives from each of the major stakeholder groups of the university (e.g., students, staff, faculty, alumni, corporations). As a result of an appreciative inquiry process,[7] teams were charged with developing strategies to achieve the following "how might we" questions:

- How might we increase the positive environment that keeps our students motivated and engaged throughout their studies?
- How might we create day-to-day experiences that are consistently positive for our students?
- How might we define and implement the behaviors associated with a culture of well-being that is lived by all stakeholders of Tecmilenio?
- How might we engage parents to become more committed to living their lives in a way that is consistent with the principles of positive organizational scholarship and positive psychology?
- How might we ensure that all subcontractors to the university interact with us according to the principles of positive organizational scholarship, positive psychology, and our ecosystem of well-being and happiness?
- How might we design and implement our culture so as to be the best place to work for staff and teachers?
- How might we define and implement a set of behaviors we expect our teachers to adopt as they interact with all our stakeholders?

- How might we develop a strong alumni network peopled with those who continue to support the school, each other, and society as a whole?
- How might we define and measure activities that align with the individual elements of our ecosystem?
- How might we ensure that teachers and staff feel a sense of responsibility for the well-being of the students?
- How might we develop positive deviance in our alumni who will challenge and lead society for the better?

A variety of positive practices were implemented in pursuit of these questions. For example, all students at Tecmilenio are now required to register for two semester-long classes: one on positive psychology and one on positive organizations. All faculty members and staff members engage in two courses on the same topics and must earn a certificate in those two areas. The campus ecosystem was redesigned so that rooms are named with positive terms (e.g., compassion room, thriving room, innovation room) rather than room numbers. The menu in the cafeteria was changed to reflect positive eating habits and physical well-being. A gratitude wall and interactive spaces were created in the central administration building. A happiness week is now sponsored for the entire Monterrey community. An alumni association was created and gathered 100 inspirational stories representing the achievement of happiness and well-being of Tecmilenio graduates. Ongoing and frequent assessments are conducted to measure the well-being and thriving of the community, the institution, and the university's members. Weekly leadership meetings are conducted to review the empirical data gathered on positive aspects of the university's functioning.

In addition, all students receive a personal coach or mentor in their first two years at Tecmilenio, and with the assistance of that personal coach, they develop a purpose-in-life statement during their first semester on campus. This statement is revised during the students' second year, and during their senior year, students put the statement into action by engaging in a full-time, 480-hour co-op (internship) project. This project requires students to create an intervention for the organization in which they conduct their co-op assignment. The intervention has two primary purposes: (1) to fulfill the student's purpose in life and (2) to apply a positive organizational change in the employing organization itself.

The results of implementing positive practices and operationalizing a positive philosophy at Tecmilenio have been dramatic. In the five years since the initiative was begun, not only has enrollment increased more than 11 percent per year, but it has reached 60,000 students as of this writing, with significant revenue growth. As a private university, Tecmilenio produced a return on investment of between 20 and 40 percent, approximately four times the return of the stock market at its best.

Table 5.1 exemplifies the results of Tecmilenio's transformation at the end of the 2018 academic year.

TABLE 5.1
Indicators of Tecmilenio's success in 2018

Outcome	Percentage
Increase in institution revenues (5 years)	1,379
Students employed in a job that fulfills their purpose in life	95
Students who recommend Tecmilenio to others (Net Promoter Score)	98
Companies that recommend the Tecmilenio internship program	98

Hector Escamilla himself became a worldwide advocate for positive leadership and positive energy. He sponsored research projects on his own campus in which outside experts investigated the practices and outcomes associated with positive leadership. He addressed associations and conferences all around the world to perpetuate the principles of positive energizing leadership. He and his university have infected multiple Mexican institutions, including the country's largest banking system, with the positive leadership message.

CONCLUSION

Many additional examples are available that document the effects of positively energizing leaders in facilitating the success of their organizations even in challenging and difficult times. In each of these examples, the success of the organization was not due solely to the leader at the top, of course; but in each case, positively energizing leadership unlocked resources that are often ignored or unmanaged. Most importantly, the focus of these leaders was on unleashing the often-untapped positive energy that resides in the organizations themselves and that can create results that no single person could dictate or direct. The kinds of innovative activities and procedures that were implemented across these and other organizations have been extraordinary and exciting. Truly, positively energizing leaders in these instances inspired members of their organizations to dream more, learn more, do more, and become more.

6
YEAH, BUTS: OBJECTIONS AND RESPONSES

Despite evidence showing that positive energy is heliotropic, that positively energizing leadership improves organizations, and that the application of positive principles appears to affect individual employees and bottomline performance for the better, skeptics still persist. Some critics have disparaged a positive focus as being unrealistic, naive, and narrow-minded.[1] This is certainly understandable in light of the current environment of racial injustice, economic devastation, and loss of life. When people are depressed, in mourning, or experiencing emotional pain, mandating that everyone think happy thoughts and be cheerful is mockery. In these cases, touting positive relational energy can be seen as inauthentic, disingenuous, dishonest, or untrustworthy—that is, as false positivity—or the exact opposite of virtuous responses to trying times.

This chapter addresses doubts, potential resistance, and misgivings sometimes expressed by individuals who encounter positive topics for the first time or who are experiencing difficult challenges. It is not unusual for leaders in organizations to respond to their exposure to positive energy, positive leadership, and positive practices with statements such as the following:

> "This is too syrupy, touchy-feely, and maudlin for my organization."
>
> "This is irrelevant to the difficult issues we face."
>
> "People in this organization would never take this seriously."
>
> "This whole approach costs too much."
>
> "This produces delusional thinking and is unrealistic."
>
> "I have difficult people to manage, and I can't be positive with them and get results."
>
> "This is a deflection from our major concerns."
>
> "I can't be easygoing and soft while maintaining the respect of my people."
>
> "This approach encourages reckless optimism."
>
> "It represents a narrow moral agenda."
>
> "This is a nice-to-do but not a need-to-do in my organization."

MAJOR AREAS OF CRITIQUE

These objections represent one reason why this book is so heavily reliant on empirical evidence that confirms the credibility of the prescriptions being offered. The objections raised by managers and executives, however, represent just one area of concern. Other critiques have been articulated by scientists, journalists, and commentators, and they can be organized into five main categories. This chapter addresses each of these criticisms and provides some rejoinders and examples. The five categories of objections are as follows:

- Research objections
- Culture and values objections
- Simplicity and narrowness objections
- Manipulation and ethical objections
- Practice and application objections

RESEARCH OBJECTIONS

The main research-related criticisms can be summarized by these statements:

- Sweeping claims are made about human nature and the causes of happiness, often based on limited studies of, mainly, college students.
- Research findings are often overstated, simplistic, and misleading. Misanalyzing data and misinterpreting or overclaiming results are common. Real proof is scarce.

It is true that much more empirical research is needed regarding positive phenomena. The entire field is still in the toddler stage of development—that is, it is beginning to get its research legs and move along independently, but it is not yet in a mature, well-developed stage of scientific inquiry. Many more questions are in need of answers than have been addressed. Thus, some of the research-based criticisms are valid and important.

On the other hand, a growing amount of published empirical research has been conducted that demonstrates the importance and impact of positive leadership and positive practices. More than 3 million publications on positive psychology and an additional 3 million publications on positive leadership are available on Google Scholar. A substantial amount of research confirms that when individuals experience positive leadership and positive relational energy and engage in positive practices, significant positive results occur.[2] Table 6.1 lists some of the confirmed outcomes that occur when individuals experience positive leadership, positive relational energy, and positive practices.

One meta-analysis of more than 500 empirical studies reported that employees in organizations with positively energizing leadership experience better health, lower absenteeism, greater self-regulation, stronger motivation, enhanced creativity, positive relationships, and lower turnover.[3] Studies investigating organizational outcomes have been fewer but have nonetheless demonstrated significant effects of positively energizing leadership on bottom-line performance. For example, research has found that financial performance, productivity, quality, and customer satisfaction improved significantly when organizations were exposed to positive leadership and positive practices.[4]

Much is left to be done, of course, and studies regarding organization outcomes are especially sparse. Nevertheless, there is substantial evidence emerging confirming that both individuals and organizations are affected by positive dynamics.

TABLE 6.1

Outcomes of experiencing positive emotions, positive relational energy, and positive practices

---

Live 11 years longer than normal
Succumb to fewer illnesses
Have higher survival rates after serious illness or accident
Stay married longer
Tolerate pain better
Work harder
Perform better on the job
Make more money over a lifetime
Display more mental acuity
Make higher-quality decisions
Are more creative and flexible in their thinking
Are more adaptive and resilient after trials and trauma
Engage in more helping behaviors
Have lower rates of all-cause mortality, fewer heart attacks,
     and higher cancer survival rates

David, S. A., Boniwell, I., & Ayers, A. C. (2013). *The Oxford handbook of happiness.* New York, NY: Oxford University Press. Also, Cameron, K. S., & Spreitzer, G. M. (2012). *The Oxford handbook of positive organizational scholarship.* New York, NY: Oxford University Press. Also, Snyder, C. R., & Lopez, S. J. (2002). *Handbook of positive psychology.* New York: Oxford University Press.

CULTURE AND VALUES OBJECTIONS

The main objections related to culture and values can be summarized as follows:

- A focus on the positive is applicable only to the existing Western socioeconomic and value systems, which emphasize individualism, capitalism, and Western definitions of thriving and happiness.

- Positivity has a white, middle-class bias and ignores the plight of minorities and disadvantaged groups. Poverty, inequality, injustice, repression, and other societal problems are ignored.

It is true that much of the original research and writing done from a positive perspective was conducted in the Western world and in the English language. A Eurocentric and U.S.-centric bias dominated the literature in the first decade or so after the field's emergence at the beginning of this millennium. However, even before the COVID pandemic of 2020, research on positive phenomena had not ignored difficult issues and negative phenomena, and research on these topics has not remained Western.

For example, as shown in table 6.2, a breadth of countries and cultures were represented at the International Positive Psychology Association (IPPA) meetings in 2017. It is evident that research on positive topics is not limited to the Western Hemisphere or to first-world countries. Table 6.3 lists the countries being studied in scientific articles presented in those meetings. Table 6.4 provides a sample of the topics being studied. Notice the variety of difficult and so-called negative, problematic topics being actively investigated and the societal problems being pursued in many non-Western countries.

The worldwide challenges brought on by issues related to health, justice, and the environment are certainly in need of increased attention. It does not appear, however, that systemic national, ethnic, or social class

TABLE 6.2
A sample of countries represented by
scholars and researchers at the IPPA
congress

Argentina	Mexico
Australia	Nepal
Austria	Netherlands
Brazil	Norway
Canada	Poland
Chile	Portugal
China	Russia
Denmark	Singapore
Finland	South Africa
France	South Korea
Germany	Spain
Iceland	Switzerland
Israel	Taiwan
Italy	United Kingdom
Japan	United States

biases are evident in the research. Numerous studies on
difficult topics such as anxiety, traumatic brain injuries,
HIV patients, poverty, and LGBT issues are being investigated through a positive lens. Much work is to be done,
of course, but evidence exists that these issues are being
investigated in earnest and are increasingly appearing in
the literature.

SIMPLICITY AND NARROWNESS OBJECTIONS

Objections related to narrowness and simplicity are similar to the biases against positive topics in general that
were highlighted above. These objections frequently

TABLE 6.3
A sample of countries used as the focus of study at the
IPPA congress

Academic achievement in Bhutan
Happiness in Chinese teens
Trust among Chinese retirees
Transforming culture in Ukraine
Optimal environments in French schools
Body image among youth in Singapore
Purpose and well-being in Hispanic women
Test construction—an Indian model
Education modules for Indian rural women
PsyCap and employability in Africa
PsyCap in Indian nongovernmental organizations
Secondary students' well-being in Singapore
Positive psychology in Europe
Buddhist mind training
Positive education in India
Gratitude: International perspectives
Positive leadership in New Zealand Customs
Intercultural studies of semantics

come from individuals who hear about positive leadership
and positive practices only superficially. Specifically:

- Positive leadership and positive practices are
  warmed-over "positive thinking" from many decades
  ago, and the focus on "happiology" is oversimplified
  and superficial. Positive writing is merely a restate-
  ment of universal rules for being happy. Life is
  complex, and concentrating only on the positive is
  wishful thinking.
- Positive leadership and positive practices imply that
  all other scholarly research is negative. Positive

TABLE 6.4

A sample of problem-based topics being investigated at the IPPA congress

---

Courage and childhood anxiety
Traumatic brain injury
Neurorehabilitation
Resilience in the military
Self-compassion in women
Positivity and disability
Values-in-Action (VIA) with forensic patients
Stress and perception
Decreased happiness among adolescents
Child psychotherapy
Social capital and academically at-risk students
Neuropsychiatric disorders in childhood
Psychosocial factors among Black HIV patients
Positivity in Parkinson's disease patients
Resilience in kidney disease patients
Racial and ethnic gaps in life satisfaction
Spiritual reframing with HIV patients
Character strengths in LGBT individuals
Hope and meaning in poverty
Embracing the dark side

---

advocates ban negativity and negative phenomena from scientific exploration and from workplace dynamics.

The foundation for positive leadership, positive relational energy, and positive practices was, in fact, established many decades ago, dating back to William James's writings on what he termed "healthy mindedness,"[5] Gordon Allport's interest in positive human characteristics,[6] Marie Jahoda's emphasis on positive mental health,[7] Abraham

Maslow's advocacy for studying healthy people in lieu of sick people,[8] Douglas McGregor's human side of enterprise,[9] and Warren Bennis's emphasis on optimism and hope.[10] Most of this earlier positively themed work, however, was not based on scientific research and empirical investigations. Instead, it largely focused on advocacy and the promotion of an approach to addressing problems, overcoming ills, and resolving difficulties.

More recently, rigorous scientific investigations have uncovered heretofore unrecognized findings that extend well beyond the early writers and a focus on happiology. For example, a variety of studies have found that brain activity is significantly affected by exposure to positive energy and positive practices.[11] More mental acuity and mental activation occur when a person is experiencing a positive condition compared with a negative condition, and so people are apt to perform better on memory, memorization, and problem-solving tasks. As mentioned in chapter 2, heart rhythms are significantly affected by exposure to the positive,[12] and so the heart beats more rhythmically when experiencing a positive state compared with a negative state, thus extending longevity. The central nervous system (including Vagus nerve health) functions most effectively when positive emotions are fostered,[13] so internal organs are healthier. Bodily rhythm coherence (an alignment of brain and heart rhythms) is at its peak when a person is experiencing positive relational energy.[14]

In addition to individual physiological benefits, positive relational energy and positive practices also affect organizations' performance. Bottom-line performance (meaning profitability, productivity, quality, innovation, customer satisfaction, and employee engagement) increases significantly when scores on positive practices improve.[15] Even within organizations where positive practices and positive energy might predictably be interpreted as too soft, syrupy, and irrelevant (e.g., financial services, the military, firms engaged in downsizing, health-care organizations, high-tech firms, or firms in the midst of a recession), performance on bottom-line indicators exceeded industry averages by a factor of 4 to 10 (see chapter 2).

It is evident that by examining research on positive practices and positive energy, new findings are emerging regularly that extend well beyond commonly accepted points of view espoused by the founders of a positive point of view. Oversimplification and superficiality do not appear to be accurate descriptors of the current state of the empirical research.

MANIPULATION AND ETHICAL OBJECTIONS

Some have criticized the research on positive leadership, positive practices, and positive energy as being manipulative of people in order to get them to work harder for the benefit of the organization or their bosses. Positive leadership, these critics say, takes unfair advantage of people and only reinforces power differentials. Specifically:

- Positive interventions manipulate clients and employees. People are made to feel good in order to coerce certain outcomes from them. Positive energy, positive practices, and positive leadership are unscrupulous techniques used to take advantage of workers.

- The values of these positive approaches are not conducive to an increase in human freedom but only to conformity.

It is true that when experiencing positive leadership and positive relational energy, individuals tend to work harder and produce outcomes at much higher levels than they would otherwise. Empirical evidence confirms that creating a positive work environment, helping employees flourish personally, and fostering a sense of value and meaningfulness at work almost always pay off in higher levels of productivity and effectiveness.

However, these arguments confuse positively energizing leadership with false positivity. Disingenuous positivity programs designed primarily to get people to work harder are contrary to the very definition of positive relational energy and positive leadership. Especially when facing trying times, mandating positivity or superimposing false positivity on a workforce is unscrupulous and will likely backfire. Rather than denigrating and crushing initiatives and opportunities for personal growth, the goal of positive leadership is to help people *dream more, learn more, do more, and become more.*

Research has found, for example, that employees are willing to trade extensive monetary benefits for meaningful work, feeling valued as individuals, and experiencing heightened well-being—all direct outcomes of positive leadership and positive relational energy. A colleague, Wayne Cascio, found that experiencing a meaningful and positive work environment is more important to employees than any other aspect of employment, including pay and rewards, opportunities for promotion, or working conditions.[16] Employees are willing to give up vacation days and a substantial percentage of their pay for meaningful work that helps them flourish. Genuine positive relational energy and positive leadership are antithetical to manipulation and coercion.

In sum, little evidence exists that helping people feel valued, feel energized, and thrive at work is an unethical, manipulative thing to do. In reality, it appears that no trade-off is necessary between helping individuals flourish and having organizations do well.

PRACTICE AND APPLICATION OBJECTIONS

The practice and application objections are the ones most frequently expressed by leaders and managers attempting to implement positive leadership and positive practices in their organizations. These issues are exemplified by the comments cited at the beginning of the chapter related to being too soft, touchy-feely, unrealistic, and not taken seriously.

A few suggestions, based on empirical research as well as numerous interventions in organizations, can help alleviate many of these concerns and build supporters rather than detractors when implementing positive leadership and fostering positive relational energy in organizations:

- *Rely on empirical evidence.* A great deal of highly credible research has been conducted that demonstrates the impact of positive leadership and positive practices on individuals and on organizations. Skeptical audiences need proof that this is not just storytelling and snake oil. Abundant research is available,[17] including that cited in chapters 2 through 5.

- *Begin with 1 percent improvements.* If an airplane takes off at Washington's Reagan International Airport and travels around the world intending to return to Washington, DC, but it is consistently off course by one degree, the plane will land in Atlanta, Georgia, to the south or in Augusta, Maine, to the north. A small change puts you in a very different place over time. Implementing positive practices need only begin with small, easy-to-implement changes.

- *Activate positive energizers.* Identify individuals in the organization that inspire and uplift others. Mobilize them as a team to expose others in the organization to positive practices and positive energy. Dramatically successful results have occurred in organizations throughout the world when positive energizers are mobilized as a group, provided resources, and given an assignment to infect their organizations with positive energy.[18]

• *Record and publicize small wins.* As individuals are made aware of good news and tiny victories, resistance wanes (it is not worth fighting against small, positive changes), momentum builds (it gives the impression that progress is being made), and support is generated (a bandwagon effect occurs and people support a winning strategy).[19] The rule is: find something easy to change, change it, and publicize it. Keep track of progress and the small victories.

• *Maintain absolute integrity.* Be honest about missteps and bloopers as well as successes. Ensure that individuals are kept informed of plans, intended changes, strategies, and consequences. Honesty is crucial when the future is ambiguous and unsettling. In a series of studies in companies, people in high-trust organizations experienced 74 percent less stress, 106 percent more energy, 50 percent higher productivity, 13 percent fewer sick days, 76 percent more engagement, and 40 percent less burnout than people in low-trust organizations.[20]

CONCLUSION

It is not surprising that resistance and criticism are associated with positive leadership, positive practices, and positive energy. The popular press, self-help gurus, and motivational speakers have popularized positive phenomena, but in so doing they have sometimes become viewed as substance-less happiology advocates.[21] As it turns out, however, individuals and organizations have been greatly advantaged by implementing and capitalizing on positive practices and positive leadership—especially positively energizing leadership. Even in the most difficult of circumstances (as in environmental crises, fiscal constraints, retrenchment, personal loss, or pandemics), empirical evidence has confirmed that positively energizing leadership produces positive results.

This evidence is crucial because none of us would subject ourselves to, for example, a physician who practiced medicine on the basis of a magazine article, an inspiring story, or an interesting example. We would need to be confident that his or her medical practice is based on credible, validated science. The same is true in organizations. Because leaders have such significant impact on the performance of organizations, it is important that when we give advice to leaders, we have evidence that what we are prescribing is credible and valid. The approach taken in this book is to provide this kind of evidence.

The conclusion, then, is the same as the assertion at the beginning of the book. At a time when earthquakes, floods, tornadoes, cyberattacks, wildfires, and the worldwide COVID-19 pandemic have created unprecedented challenges; where racial injustice, economic devastation, and loss of life have elevated our collective consciousness regarding what is wrong in our world; where contention, outrage, and violence have become ubiquitous; and where extensive economic, emotional, and health consequences have resulted in dramatic changes in normal daily activities, relationships, institutions, and even values, it is difficult to be positive. Happiology is not exactly a preferred prescription for coping with tragedy.

That is why the key message of this book is different from merely prescribing positivity as a panacea. It relies on empirical evidence to reinforce a threefold conclusion. First, *all human beings are inclined toward and flourish in the presence of positive energy.* This is called the heliotropic effect, and it begins in infancy.[22] Individuals and organizations will flourish in the presence of positive energy, especially as demonstrated by leadership. However, because bad is often stronger than good,[23] human beings have learned to ignore the positive and pay more attention to the negative. Building and reinforcing positive relational energy, therefore, is paramount for effectively addressing the difficulties and challenges we face, especially in these trying times.

Second, *positive relational energy is best created through virtuous actions,* particularly as demonstrated by leaders. Positively energizing leaders characterized by virtuous behavior have been found to produce extraordinary results. This prescription is not advocating that leaders merely generate a positive *attitude,* but rather that genuine action be taken that is directed at helping other people flourish. Most particularly, virtuousness in the forms of generosity, altruism, and contribution; gratitude, recognition, and humility; and trust, integrity, and honesty has been shown to create significant and positive impact on organizations and their employees, with performance often substantially above industry norms.

Third, *both organizations and individuals perform at a significantly higher level when virtuousness and positive relational energy are fostered.* The irony is that virtuous actions do not need to produce desirable outcomes in order to be valuable. Virtuousness is, by definition, its own reward, pursued for its own sake. Virtuousness represents the best of the human condition and leads to positive relational energy—a life-giving force. When people are struggling emotionally, grieving from the loss of loved ones, jobs, or relationships, or just gritting through difficult days, virtuous actions are not only a universal balm but a way to turn trying times into flourishing times.

CONCLUSION
Principles and Action Implications

Now that you have learned about forms of energy, the heliotropic effect, how positively energizing leadership affects the performance of organizations and their employees, and how to recognize and develop positive energizers, a final question remains: So what? What are the action implications associated with the discussions contained in the previous chapters?

In this concluding chapter, several principles are summarized along with suggestions for taking action. The question is, What are the behavioral implications of positively energizing leadership?

• *PRINCIPLE*: In trying times—including the recent spate of earthquakes, floods, tornadoes, cyberattacks, ethical lapses, wildfires, and the worldwide COVID-19 pandemic—most people tend to focus on the uncomfortable, the uncertainty, and the adversities. Racial injustice, economic devastation, and loss of life have elevated our consciousness toward what is wrong in our world. When people are struggling emotionally, stressed from the loss of loved ones, jobs, or relationships, or just gritting through difficult days, it is hard to be positive. Happiology is not the preferred prescription for coping with tragedy.

SUGGESTION: Focus less on mere cheerfulness, positive thinking, and unbridled optimism than on demonstrating virtuousness. Virtuous behaviors—including gratitude, humility, kindness, generosity, contribution, forgiveness, compassion, trust, and integrity—are heliotropic and lead to positive energy and thriving, especially in difficult times. Behaving virtuously provides a way to flourish in trying times by unlocking the positive energy inherent in all human beings.

• *PRINCIPLE*: A variety of forms of energy exist, including physical energy, emotional energy, mental energy, and relational energy. Each of the first three forms of energy diminishes with use. They require recuperation or recovery time when expended. Relational energy actually elevates with use. It is renewing.

SUGGESTION: Nurture relational energy with people close to you. Make certain that you invest sufficient time and resources in these relationships so that they remain elevating, replenishing, and life-giving. Inspire these people to dream more, learn more, do more, and become more by demonstrating positively energizing leadership.

• *PRINCIPLE*: Every living system—from single-cell organisms to complex human beings—is inclined toward positive energy and away from negative energy, or toward that which enhances life and away from that which detracts from life. This is called the heliotropic effect, and abundant scientific evidence confirms its presence in human beings.

SUGGESTION: Capitalize on the heliotropic effect in your leadership roles, in your relationships, in your marriage, in your work, and with your children. Enhance and engender life more than you detract from life. Be a source of thriving for other people by behaving in ways that are virtuous.

• *PRINCIPLE*: Positively energizing leadership is not the same as being extroverted, outgoing, or charismatic or possessing a senior position in the organization. Individuals lower in the hierarchy can be the most positively energizing people in the organization.

SUGGESTION: Regardless of your title or hierarchical position in your organization, give life to the system and to everyone with whom you interact. Seldom are the most positively energizing people in organizations the folks who occupy top positions. Behave virtuously toward others. Contribute to the well-being of those around you. Identify the meaningfulness of the contributions you are making.

• *PRINCIPLE:* In organizations, information and influence are frequently the primary means used by leaders to obtain results. Ensuring that employees are informed and influenced to achieve goals and targets is a central focus in most organizations. Yet, positive relational energy is significantly more important in predicting performance than are information and influence.

SUGGESTION: Contribute more positive energy to your organizations (work, family, community, faith groups) than you extract. Give significant time and attention to enhancing positive relational energy around those with whom you interact—more than the time you spend giving instructions or attempting to influence others. Consciously strive to be a positively energizing leader. Capitalize on the positively energizing people in your work and in your life.

• *PRINCIPLE*: Positive energizers are higher performers than other people, and other people perform at higher levels when they are around positive energizers. Positive energizers help other people flourish without expecting a reward or recognition.

SUGGESTION: Identify the positive energizers in your organization and in your relationships. Spend time with these people, reflect their energy back to them, and mobilize them to help foster organizational change. Put together a team of positive energizers to lead important change initiatives.

• *PRINCIPLE*: In chaotic, turbulent, uncertain conditions, a stable standard must be identified in order to effectively manage the environment. Without a constant, unwavering guidepost, it is impossible to make progress. Something universal must be identified to guide behavior.

SUGGESTION: A universally accepted standard is the value of virtuousness. All human beings value kindness over abuse, generosity over selfishness, trust over distrust, love over hate, and compassion over indifference. In addition, virtuousness is heliotropic, and from infancy all human beings are inclined toward and flourish in the presence of virtuousness. Prioritize the demonstration of virtuousness, especially when others are struggling with uncertainty, contention, or grief.

• *PRINCIPLE*: Because bad is stronger than good—that is, negative events create a larger and more immediate reaction than positive events—most of us pay a great deal of attention to problems, challenges, and obstacles. Most case studies in courses and most agenda items in meetings challenge us to solve problems and overcome obstacles. We mostly address deficit gaps, or the gap between poor performance and acceptable performance.

SUGGESTION: At some point, address abundance gaps, or the gap between acceptable performance and positively deviant, extraordinary performance. Spend some time on what is going right, what helps people flourish, and how you can achieve extraordinarily positive outcomes. Celebrate what is life-giving. As a leader, spend time pursuing spectacular performance and striving for your highest aspirations, not just solving problems. Aim for positive deviance.

• *PRINCIPLE*: Contribution goals affect performance much more powerfully than achievement goals. An inherent tendency exists in all human beings toward generosity, contribution, and kindness, and all people respond, eventually, to these conditions. Generosity is a better predictor of our own well-being and performance than what we receive from others.

SUGGESTION: Spend some time engaged in activities that produce a benefit that outlasts your lifetime, that produce a benefit to others without expectation that you will receive a return, and that reinforce the inherent virtuousness of those around you. The contributions you make will far outlast your personal achievements.

• *PRINCIPLE*: Expressing gratitude is associated with better personal health, performance, and well-being as well as affecting the recipient's well-being, physical health, and performance. Similarly, demonstrating humility—accurately viewing oneself, appreciating others, and being willing to learn from others—is closely related to gratitude and is associated with similar outcomes. Leadership humility and expressions of gratitude go hand in hand.

SUGGESTION: Don't go a day without expressing gratitude to someone else. Keep a gratitude journal. Write down three things each day for which you are grateful. Regularly write gratitude notes or letters to others. Willingly seek feedback and use it to improve your own leadership behavior; thank those who provide the feedback.

• *PRINCIPLE*: Trust lies at the core of human biological development from the day an infant is born. As individuals mature, trust becomes a critical feature in the development of positively energizing relationships. All successful relationships and all organizational performance are based on the presence of trust.

SUGGESTION: Ensure that your word is your bond. Tell the truth. Maintain your standards even when no one is looking. Ensure that you are consistent, dependable, and authentic in your relationships with others, especially in your leadership roles. Make more deposits than withdrawals in the emotional bank account associated with your relationships.

• *PRINCIPLE*: A majority of books on leadership rely on storytelling, inspirational events, top-10 lists, or personal experience to convey leadership advice. Although these are often uplifting, insightful, and inspirational, empirical evidence is usually absent. The validity and credibility of leadership prescriptions are rarely reported.

SUGGESTION: Seek evidence of credibility, validity, and legitimacy associated with leadership advice. As with the development of a coronavirus vaccine, there should be scientific evidence that what is being prescribed actually produces the desired outcomes. Ensure that your leadership practice is consistent with the scientific evidence.

• *PRINCIPLE*: If an airplane takes off from Washington's Reagan International Airport and travels around the world intending to return to Washington, DC, but it is consistently off course by one degree, the plane will land south of Atlanta or north of Bangor, Maine. A small change puts you in a very different place over time.

SUGGESTION: Continue to identify 1 percent improvements that you will implement and stick with. You will end up with substantially enhanced performance over time. Opt for a small, consistent change rather than pursuing a revolution or complete transformation.

• *PRINCIPLE*: According to the NTL Institute, you will remember approximately 5 percent of what you hear in classes, lectures, or podcasts, approximately 10 percent of what you read, and approximately 20 percent of what you see and experience. However, you will remember approximately 90 percent of what you teach.

SUGGESTION: Share your learning and insights from this book with other people. Be a lifelong teacher. Contribute to others' learning, because you were privileged to gain insights or ideas that can lead to improvement. Help other people flourish. Remember, if your actions inspire others to dream more, learn more, do more, and become more, you are a positively energizing leader.

By way of wrap-up, here are a few anecdotal testimonials from leaders who have put the suggestions in this chapter into practice. The quotations illustrate the application of these positive practices in a variety of situations and circumstances.

From a senior executive in a large, multinational financial services organization:

[Our CEO] wanted to implement something that would make the people feel inspired to do their best work and to feel valued. . . . We believed that by demonstrating positively energizing leadership and positive practices we could do all of these things simultaneously: create value for our people, create value for our customers, and create value for our shareholders.

From a senior executive in a health-care organization that was facing a fiscal crisis:

We are in a very competitive health care market, so we have had to differentiate ourselves through our compassionate and caring culture. . . . I know it sounds trite, but we really do love our patients. . . . People love working here, and our employees' family members love us too. . . . Even when we downsized, our CEO maintained the highest levels of integrity. He told the truth, and he shared everything. He got the support of everyone by his genuineness, personal concern, and positive leadership. . . . It wasn't hard to feel energized.

From a graduate of a prestigious MBA program:

This summer after graduation, I chose to undergo a preventive double mastectomy and breast reconstruction—not your typical post-MBA plans. A few years ago, I found out that I had the BRCA1 gene mutation and an 88 percent chance of having breast cancer in my lifetime. My mother and grandmother, who also have the BRCA1 mutation, were diagnosed with breast cancer when they were in their early 30s. As a woman in my late 20s, I felt the timing was right to take a pre-emptive strike against breast cancer with this procedure. Little did I know that my time in my MBA program would impact this experience. . . . In my MBA program I learned about positive practices and positive energy. I started to think: How could I approach this experience, something that could be seen as terrible and traumatizing, with a positive approach? How could I maintain a positive perspective during the three-month reconstruction and recovery process, and how could I leverage this experience to have a positive impact on others? . . . Six weeks after my surgery and 10 blog posts later, I can tell you that the positive approach I learned in my graduate program dramatically affected my recovery. While it was not the best summer of my life and there were a couple of not-so-great weeks, my overall recovery has been better than expected and I'm very happy with my decision. Most importantly, other young women with the BRCA1 gene have already reached out to me after seeing my blog. Knowing that I am helping others has been incredibly fulfilling.

 # RESOURCES

Measuring Positive Energy

Knowing who the positive energizers and de-energizers are is a major advantage. Creating teams of positive energizers, for example, can markedly impact the success of organizational change efforts. Energizers help others sign up for change initiatives and diminish their resistance. Similarly, positive energizers can coach and mentor other organization members, and they can help individuals who are less positively energizing to become substantially more so. A variety of assessment tools are available for identifying positively energizing individuals. These assessment alternatives can also be used to help coach or mentor individuals preparing for leadership positions.

1. CREATING AN ENERGY NETWORK MAP

The most sophisticated method for identifying positive energizers in an organization is to create a network map of all possible relationships. This is done by creating a list of every person in the organization. Each person in the organization responds to the following question regarding each other person on the list: When I interact with this person, what happens to my energy? That is, to what extent am I enthused, elevated, and uplifted when I interact with this person? Responses are graded on the following scale:

7—I am very positively energized when I interact with this person

6—I am moderately positively energized when I interact with this person

5—I am slightly positively energized when I interact with this person

4—I am neither energized nor de-energized when I interact with this person

3—I am slightly de-energized when I interact with this person

2—I am moderately de-energized when I interact with this person

1—I am very de-energized when I interact with this person

Having each person rate his or her energizing connection with every other person in the group produces a set of ratings associated with each person's name. These ratings are entered into a network mapping statistical program (there are many available online), and the program creates a network map based on relational energy—that is, the energy exchanged when two people interact (see figure R.1). You can determine which individuals have the most energizing connections relative to others (who are in the center of a network map) and which individu-

FIGURE R.1

An illustration of energy density

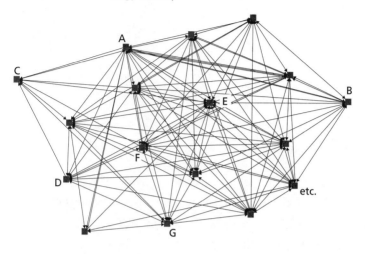

als have fewer energizing connections (who are on the periphery of the network map). (See chapter 2.)

You can also match positive energizers with hierarchical levels, functions, locations, and other relevant information. These data provide information about the relative amount of energizing that is occurring in the entire organization. In figure R.1, the measure of energy density is 70 percent (that is, 70 percent of all pairwise connections are positively energizing), a relatively dense energy network.

2. CREATING A BUBBLE CHART

When the objective is to identify the positive energizers in the organization in a short amount of time, simply ask

A bubble chart of energy ratings

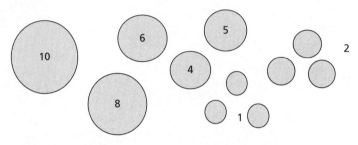

all members of the group to confidentially write the names of the two or three most positively energizing people in the group. (More names can be listed in large groups.) Have each person hand in a slip of paper or email the two or three names to you. Then, count the number of nominations that each person receives. Create a bubble chart showing different-sized bubbles with the largest bubbles displaying those with the largest number of nominations and the smallest bubbles showing the smallest number of nominations (see figure R.2). The results can usually be shown anonymously, with numbers rather than names in the bubbles. This avoids embarrassing or deflating individuals in the organization, but allows the leader to get a good sense of who the energizing people are. (See chapter 2.)

3. A PULSE SURVEY

A pulse survey is intended to monitor the overall energy levels of an organization over time (see figure R.3). Em-

FIGURE R.3

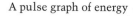

A pulse graph of energy

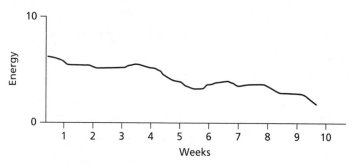

ployees are asked on a weekly basis (or more frequently) the following question: On a scale of 1 to 10, what is your energy today? The energy of employees is monitored on a regular basis using a one-question email to get a picture of the collective energy of the organization. (See chapter 2.)

If energy scores are changing—either up or down—the pulse survey plot can help guide diagnoses regarding what is going well, what factors are affecting scores, and what impact this has on bottom-line results.

4. ASSESSING POSITIVE ENERGIZER BEHAVIORS

It is often helpful to assess the extent to which individuals are displaying the key attributes of positively energizing leadership. This information can be used for developmental and coaching purposes as well as for self-improvement purposes. Individuals can use the instrument to rate themselves, but usually the instrument is used by members of an organization to rate their leader (see figure R.4). The intent is to identify the positively energizing behaviors being displayed at work. Average scores on each item are provided below so that comparisons can be made with 600 other mid- to senior-level leaders (see figure R.5). (See chapter 3.)

Instructions: Please rate the leader of your organization using the 10-point scale below. Circle the number that best represents his or her behavior and demeanor. If the statement on the right is perfectly descriptive, circle 1. If the statement on the left is perfectly descriptive, circle 10. Use other numbers if the statements on either end are not quite accurate. A rating of 5 indicates that neither statement is descriptive.

To make sense of the resulting scores in this instrument, it may be helpful to compare them with the average scores produced by approximately 600 midlevel and senior executives. This information helps answer the question: Are my scores above or below the average of other executives?

These comparison data are an aggregation of 600 respondents who live in the United States, of whom 54 percent are female, 46 percent are male, and 89 percent hold university postgraduate degrees. A majority of organizations in which these respondents work are in the for-profit sector. These 15 attributes are very strongly related to successful organizational performance. More specifically, statistically significant associations exist between the 15 attributes and the organizational performance indicators at the $p < .001$ level (profitability, productivity,

FIGURE R.4

Assessing positive energy behaviors

ENERGIZERS		DE-ENERGIZERS
1. Helps other people flourish without expecting a payback.	10 9 8 7 6 5 4 3 2 1	1. Ensures that he or she gets the credit.
2. Expresses gratitude and humility.	10 9 8 7 6 5 4 3 2 1	2. Is selfish and resists feedback.
3. Instills confidence and self-efficacy in others.	10 9 8 7 6 5 4 3 2 1	3. Doesn't create opportunities for others to be recognized.
4. Smiles frequently.	10 9 8 7 6 5 4 3 2 1	4. Is somber and seldom smiles.
5. Forgives weaknesses in others.	10 9 8 7 6 5 4 3 2 1	5. Induces guilt or shame in others.
6. Invests in developing personal relationships	10 9 8 7 6 5 4 3 2 1	6. Doesn't invest in personal relationships.
7. Shares plum assignments and recognizes others' involvement.	10 9 8 7 6 5 4 3 2 1	7. Keeps the best for himself or herself.
8. Listens actively and empathetically.	10 9 8 7 6 5 4 3 2 1	8. Dominates the conversation and asserts his or her ideas.
9. Solves problems.	10 9 8 7 6 5 4 3 2 1	9. Creates problems.
10. Mostly sees opportunities.	10 9 8 7 6 5 4 3 2 1	10. Mostly sees roadblocks and is critical.

(*Continued*)

FIGURE R.4

Assessing positive energy behaviors (*Continued*)

ENERGIZERS		DE-ENERGIZERS
11. Clarifies meaningfulness and inspires others.	10 9 8 7 6 5 4 3 2 1	11. Is indifferent and uncaring.
12. Is trusting and trustworthy.	10 9 8 7 6 5 4 3 2 1	12. Is skeptical and lacks integrity.
13. Is genuine and authentic.	10 9 8 7 6 5 4 3 2 1	13. Is superficial and insincere.
14. Motivates others to exceed performance standards.	10 9 8 7 6 5 4 3 2 1	14. Is satisfied with mediocrity or "good enough."
15. Mobilizes positive energizers who can motivate others.	10 9 8 7 6 5 4 3 2 1	15. Ignores energizers who are eager to help.

quality, employee morale, customer satisfaction). This means that the probability that the relationship between positively energizing leadership and the performance of the organization occurs by chance is less than 1 in 1,000. The amount of variance accounted for (designated as R^2) ranges between 4.4 percent for financial strength and 13 percent for productivity, employee morale, and customer satisfaction. Many factors determine the outcomes associated with organizations, of course, but the variance accounted for by the performance criteria being measured—productivity, quality, morale, customer satisfaction, and financial strength—indicates that positively energizing leadership is an important factor.

FIGURE R.5

Mean scores for the positive energy behaviors assessment

1	4.74
2	5.37
3	5.47
4	5.88
5	5.57
6	5.14
7	5.48
8	5.60
9	5.96
10	5.93
11	5.79
12	5.90
13	5.83
14	5.89
15	5.88

5. IDENTIFYING POSITIVE ENERGIZERS THROUGH INTERVIEWS

Identifying and hiring positive energizers is often a high priority if organizational performance is to improve and reach the highest levels possible. Positive energizers get better results than average employees. To identify candidates who might be positively energizing leaders in the organization, consider using the following interview questions. The questions are intended to determine the extent to which individuals have experienced positive energy, have helped other people experience it, and have achieved positively deviant (extraordinarily positive) performance for themselves and with others. (See chapter 3.)

- *Describe an organization you've worked for that you've fallen in love with. What was it about this organization that caused you to love it? What did you learn?*
- *Describe a role you've had that you absolutely loved. Describe why you fell in love with it. What did you learn?*
- *Describe a project, a work experience, or a challenging situation that exemplifies when you have done your best work. Describe this situation or challenge. What contributed to your success? What did you learn? If you could do it all over again, what would you do differently?*
- *Describe the best leadership or management team you've ever been a part of. What made this team so special? What did you learn?*
- *Describe the best leader you've worked with or worked for. What made this leader so special? What did you learn from this person? What is one gift from this person that you carry with you today?*
- *Describe a situation in which a coworker or employee needed your assistance to succeed or flourish. How did you help this person achieve his or her highest potential? What did you learn?*
- *Describe a time when you achieved peak performance, when you have been at your best, or when*

you have become positively deviant. What did you do? What did you learn?

6. RATING POSITIVELY ENERGIZING LEADERS

A quick and simple way to evaluate positively energizing leaders is to use this short, five-question assessment (Owens et al., 2016). Employees simply rate their leader on these five attributes, each of which characterizes their impressions of the leader. The question is, To what extent is the leader of this organization a positive leader? A 7-point Likert response scale can be used, ranging from 7 (very typical of this leader) to 1 (very atypical of this leader).

- *I feel invigorated when I interact with this person.*
- *After interacting with this person, I feel more energy to do my work.*
- *I feel increased vitality when I interact with this person.*
- *I would go to this person when I need to be "pepped up."*
- *After an exchange with this person, I feel more stamina to do my work.*

Aggregating the responses of employees in a particular business unit or team provides a mean score. This score does not identify the specific behaviors being displayed by the leader of a unit (as in assessment #4 above), but it does provide a quick way to determine the extent to which employees are being positively energized by their leader. (See chapter 3.)

Examples of Activities and Practices

SOME PRACTICES USED BY POSITIVELY ENERGIZING LEADERS

- **Reflected Best-Self Feedback Process**
  - A personal feedback tool that provides descriptive stories of individuals' best selves—when they created extraordinary value. This results in a best-self portrait and action plans designed to capitalize on personal strengths. (See https://positiveorgs.bus.umich.edu/tools)

- **90-in-90 Challenge**
  - A tool to identify members for a positive energizer team and provide them with a challenge to infect 90 percent of the organization with positive leadership in 90 days. Provide a day's training in advance regarding tools and practices.

- **Personal Management Interview Process**
  - A practice based on one-on-one meetings between managers and their direct reports designed to foster continuous improvement, accountability for

performance, feedback, and developing employees into extraordinary performers. (See chapter 6 of Cameron, 2012.)

- **Supportive Communication**
  - ◦ A technique for delivering corrective or negative feedback in ways that foster stronger, more collaborative relationships. (See chapter 4.)

- **Engagement of Employees**
  - ◦ Practices that foster high levels of engagement among employees by managing ideological capital, social capital, intellectual capital, and financial capital. (See chapter 8 of Cameron, 2020.)

- **Empowerment of Employees**
  - ◦ A set of practices for enhancing the empowerment of employees through self-efficacy, self-determination, personal consequence, personal meaning, and trust. (See chapter 8 of Cameron, 2020.)

- **Customer Loyalty**
  - ◦ Practices for diagnosing levels of customer commitment and helping to create lifelong customer loyalty through identifying basic, performance, and surprise-and-delight criteria.

- **Everest Goals**
  - ◦ A tool for identifying organizational and individual goals that extends beyond normal SMART goal setting and leads to extraordinary levels of achievement. (See chapter 5 of Cameron, 2013.)

- **Reciprocity Ring**
  - A tool used to create a network of contributions in which members of an organization acquire assistance and resources that were previously unknown and/or unacknowledged. (See giveandtakeinc.com/Givitas)

- **Gratitude Journals and Gratitude Visits**
  - A variety of practices to help individuals experience a gratitude condition daily as well as to experience the impact of a profound interaction based on thanksgiving.

- **Rule of Five**
  - An exercise in which the team identifies five customers to wow and five customers to fire.

- **Value-Added and Needed**
  - An exercise in which members of a team provide feedback to one another and receive commitments regarding highly valued individual contributions and what else is needed to reach positively deviant results.

PRACTICES USED BY THE BUSINESS AND FINANCE DIVISION AT THE UNIVERSITY OF MICHIGAN

POSITIVE MEETINGS
- Formal presentations at all-staff meetings
- Small monthly group meetings
- One-on-one meetings
- Sharing in huddles
- Adding positive culture agenda items at team meetings

POSITIVE COMMUNICATION

- Daily positive message in staff communications
- Slack channels
- Newsletters
- Weekly emails
- Positivity weekly messages
- Weekly video updates
- "Getting to know you" posts with photos
- "Thoughts for Thursday"
- Sharing what's "going right"
- Feedback sessions
- "Positive point" time

POSITIVE DISPLAYS

- Positivity boards
- Gratitude boards
- "Happy thoughts"
- Quotes
- Gratitude tree
- Question of the week
- "Positive energy wall"
- Positive tips
- Brain teasers
- Compliments compiled into a paper doll for each employee
- Work resolutions
- Utilizing video boards
- Personal purpose boards
- Commitment cards with 1 percent change displayed on desk

POSITIVE ACTIVITIES/EVENTS

- Puzzles, quizzes, board games
- Valentines for B&F staff
- Ten-minute mindfulness, breathing exercises
- Ten-minute movement breaks
- Team raffles
- Team games
- Community nonprofit project
- March Madness
- "Getting to know" staff activity
- Healthy activities/events (meditation/yoga)
- Gratitude exercises, jar, mailboxes
- Icebreakers
- Thank-you card station
- Suggestion box
- Volunteer events
- Tours of campus
- Awards show
- Inclusive CPR/AED training

POSITIVE TREATS

- Sweet treats
- Encourage "mints"
- Potlucks (with and without competitions)
- Kick-off lunches
- Pizza
- Breakfast
- Sweet & salty event
- Pair & share lunches

PASS THE POSITIVITY/RECOGNITION

- Gratitude journals
- Rocks with positive messages
- Incentives (hard hats with stickers)
- Parker the Positive Monkey (someone does something nice for the current recipient)
- Sticky-note gratitude exercise
- 1 percent posters
- 1 percent buttons
- "You've been energized" bags with treats and team information/achievements
- Handwritten notes
- "Bright Spot" peer acknowledgment
- Employee nomination for service award
- Recognizing birthdays, milestones

See additional practices and activities described in chapter 5.

Discussion Questions

As you teach about positive relational energy, virtuousness, and the heliotropic effect, it is often helpful to consider questions that can serve as reminders of key principles or assessments of comprehension. The following discussion questions are provided to help you examine your own understanding as well as to clarify for others that you coach or teach some of the key concepts and practices that apply to positively energizing leadership. Most importantly, the questions may prompt you to act in ways that help you apply the principles and practices in this book.

1. What are the most effective ways to enhance positive relational energy in a team, a family, or an organization?

2. In trying times, what are the differences between approaches leading to positive attitudes and thinking and approaches leading to positive relational energy?

3. In what ways can individuals and organizations take advantage of the heliotropic effect?

4. What are the most notable attributes of the positive energizers you know, and how would you help someone (for example, your children or close friends) become more positively energizing?

5. In what ways is positive energy diminished, and in what ways is it strengthened, in your own relationships?

6. What are the universal, stable, unalterable standards by which you navigate your life, or your organization?

7. How do you reconcile the seeming conflict between the fact that "bad is stronger than good" and the fact that an inherent tendency toward positive energy exists in all human beings?

8. In your own life, or in the organizations to which you belong, what are examples of some abundance gaps?

9. What activities do you, or your organization, pursue that produce outcomes that will outlast a lifetime?

10. What activities do you, or your organization, pursue that provide a benefit to others without any recognition, reward, or acknowledgment?

11. What gratitude, recognition, and humility practices have been embedded in your organization, or in your own life?

12. What generous, altruistic, and contribution practices have been embedded in your organization, or in your own life?

13. What has been done in your own organization, or in your own life, that has enhanced trust, integrity, and honesty?

14. How do you manage the black holes—the people who are negative, divisive, solemn, caustic, and abrasive—in your life or in your organization?

15. What are the most effective ways you encounter issues related to diversity, equity, and inclusion in your organization?

# NOTES

Introduction

1. Christoforou, P. S., & Ashforth, B. E. (2014). Revisiting the debate on the relationship between display rules and performance: Considering the explicitness of display rules. *Journal of Applied Psychology, 100,* 249–261. Also, Abramowitz, J. A., Tolin, D. F., & Street, G. P. (2001). Paradoxical effects of thought suppression: A meta-analysis of controlled studies. *Clinical Psychology Review, 21,* 683–703. Also, Frantz, T. T., Trolley, B. C., & Farrell, M. M. (1998). Positive aspects of grief. *Pastoral Psychology, 47,* 3–17.

2. Aneja, S. (2014). *Happiology: The science of creating your happiness.* Denver, CO: Outskirts Press.

3. Grandey, A., Foo, S. C., Groth, M., & Goodwin, R. E. (2012). Free to be you and me: A climate of authenticity alleviates burnout from emotional labor. *Journal of Occupational Health Psychology, 17,* 1–14. Also, Konnikova, M. (2016, July 30). What makes people feel upbeat at work. *The New Yorker.* https://www.newyorker.com/science/maria-konnikova/what-makes-people-feel-upbeat-at-work.

4. Frantz, T. T., Trolley, B. C., & Farrell, M. M. (1998). Positive aspects of grief. *Pastoral Psychology, 47,* 3–17. Also, Stroebe, M., Stroebe, W., & Hansson, R. (1988). Bereavement research: An historical introduction. *Journal of Social Issues, 44,* 1–18. Also, Yancey, D., Greger, H., & Coburn, P. (1990). Determinants of grief resolution in cancer death. *Journal of Palliative Care, 6,* 24–31.

5. Personal communication with John Kim, May 2006.

6. Vanette, D., & Cameron, K. S. (2015). *Implementing positive organizational scholarship at Prudential.* Center for Positive Organizations, Ann Arbor: University of Michigan.

7. Hepach, R., & Warneken, F. (2018). Editorial review: Early development of prosocial behaviour: Revealing the foundation of human prosociality. *Current Opinion in Psychology, 20,* iv–vii. Also, Roth-Hanania, R., Davidov, M., & Zahn-Waxler, C. (2011). Empathy development from 8 to 16 months: Early signs of concern for others. *Infant Behavior and Development, 34,* 447–458. Also, Van de Vondervoort, J., & Hamlin, J. K. (2018). The early emergence of sociomoral evaluation: Infants prefer prosocial others. *Current Opinion in Psychology, 20,* 77–81.

8. Thomas, A. (1988). Does leadership make a difference to organizational performance? *Administrative Science Quarterly, 33*(3), 388–400. Also, Cameron, K. S. (2012). *Positive leadership: Strategies for extraordinary performance.* San Francisco, CA: Berrett-Koehler.

9. Thomas, A. (1988). Does leadership make a difference to organizational performance? *Administrative Science Quarterly, 33*(3), 388–400. Also, Lieberson, S., & O'Connor, J. (1972). Leadership and organizational performance: A study of large corporations. *American Sociological Review, 37*(2), 117–130. Also, Beck, R., & Harter, J. (2015, April 21). Managers account for 70% of variance in employee engagement. *Gallup Business Journal.* https://news.gallup.com/business journal/182792/managers-account-variance-employee-engagement .aspx.

10. Personal communication with Jim Mallozzi, September 2012.

Chapter 1

1. Smith, J. C., & Baker, H. D. (1960). Conditioning in the horseshoe crab. *Journal of Comparative and Physiological Psychology, 53,* 279–281. Also, D'Amato, M. R., & Jagoda, H. (1962). Effect of early exposure to photic stimulation on brightness discrimination and exploratory behavior. *Journal of Genetic Psychology, 101,* 267ff. Also, Mrosovsky, N., & Kingsmill, S. F. (1985). How turtles find the sea. *Zeitschrift Fur Tierpsychologie-Journal of Comparative Ethology, 67,* 237–256.

2. Heaphy, E., & Dutton, J. (2008). Positive social interactions and the human body at work: Linking organizations and physiology. *Academy of Management Review, 33,* 137–162. Also, Dutton, J. E. (2003). *Energize your workplace: How to build and sustain high-quality connections at work.* San Francisco, CA: Jossey-Bass. Also,

Erhard-Seibold, E. V. (1937). The heliotrope tradition. *Orisis, 3,* 22–46.

3. Einstein, A. (1905). Concerning an heuristic point of view toward the emission and transformation of light. *Annalen der Physik, 17,* 132–148.

4. Nightingale, F. (1860). *Notes on nursing: What it is and what it is not* (2nd ed.). London, England: Harrison (p. 44).

5. Morholt, E., Bradwein, P. F., & Joseph, A. (1966). *A sourcebook for the biological sciences.* New York, NY: Harcourt, Brace, and World, Inc. Also see Johnston, E. S. (1931). Phototropism. In Abbot, C. G. (Ed.) *Smithsonian Scientific Series* (Vol. 11). New York, NY: Smithsonian Institution Series. And, Romanes, C. J. (1893). Experiments in heliotropism. *Proceedings of the Royal Society of London, 54,* 333–335.

6. Loeb, J., & Northrop, J. H. (1917). Heliotropic animals as photometers on the basis of the validity of the Bunsen-Roscoe Law for heliotropic reactions. *National Academy of Sciences, 3*(9), 539–544.

7. Northrop, J. H., & Loeb, J. (1923). The photochemical basis of animal heliotropism. *Journal of General Physiology, 5,* 581–595.

8. Doidge, N. (2016). *The brain's way of healing.* New York, NY: Penguin Books (p. 119).

9. Martinek, K., & Berezin, I. V. (1979). Artificial light-sensitive enzymatic systems as chemical amplifiers of weak light signals. *Photochemistry and Photobiology, 29,* 637–650.

10. Doidge, N. (2016). *The brain's way of healing.* New York, NY: Penguin Books (pp. 116–117).

11. Isobe, Y., & Nishino, H. (2004). Signal transmission from the suprachiasmatic nucleus to the pineal gland via the paraventricular nucleus: Analyzed from arg-vasopressin peptide, rPer2mRNA and AVPmRNA changes in pineal AA-NATmRNA after melatonin injection during light and dark periods. *Brain Research, 1013,* 204–211.

12. Doidge, N. (2016). *The brain's way of healing.* New York, NY: Penguin Books (p. 140).

13. For example, Hamblin, M. R. (2018). Photobiomodulation for traumatic brain injury and stroke. *Journal of Neuroscience Research, 96*(4), 731–743. Hamblin, M. R. (2017). Ultraviolet irradiation of blood: "The cure that time forgot?" *Advanced Experimental Medical Biology, 996,* 295–309. Xia, Y., Gupta, G. K., Castano, A. P., Mroz, P., Avci, P., and Hamblin, M. R. (2014). CpG oligodeoxynucleotide as immune

adjuvant enhances photodynamic therapy response in murine metastatic breast cancer. *Journal of Biophotonics, 7*(11–12), 897–905.

14. Gyory, H. (2008). Medicine in ancient Egypt. In H. Selin (Ed.), *Encyclopedia of the history of science, technology, and medicine in non-Western cultures* (2nd ed., pp. 1508–1518). New York, NY: Springer. Also, Walch, J. M., Rabin, B. A., Day, R., Williams, J. N., Choi, K., Kang, J. D. (2005). The effect of sunlight on postoperative analgesic medication use: A prospective study of patients undergoing surgery. *Psychosomatic Medicine, 67,* 157–163.

15. Thompson, C. (2019, September). Out of the shadows: The impacts of light on human health. *Lighting Newswire, 233,* 69–77.

16. Baker, W. (2019). Emotional energy, relational energy, and organizational energy: Toward a multilevel model. *Annual Review of Organizational Psychology and Organizational Behavior, 6,* 373–395.

17. Quinn, R. W., Spreitzer, G. M., & Lam, C. F. (2012). Building a sustainable model of human energy in organizations: Exploring the critical role of resources. *Academy of Management Annals, 6,* 1–60.

18. Brown, C. G. (1999). *The energy of life: The science of what makes our minds and bodies work.* New York, NY: Free Press.

19. Cole, M. S., Bruch, H., & Vogel, B. (2011). Energy at work: A measurement validation and linkage to unit effectiveness. *Journal of Organizational Behavior, 33,* 445–467.

20. Williams, D. A. (2016). Cognitive-behavioral therapy in central sensitivity syndromes. *Current Rheumatology Review, 12,* 2–12.

21. Pressman, S. D., Jenkins, B., & Moskowitz, J. (2019). Positive affect and health: What do we know and where next should we go? *Annual Review of Psychology, 70,* 627–650. Also, Pressman, S. D., & Cohen, S. (2012). Positive emotion words and longevity in famous deceased psychologists. *Health Psychology, 31,* 297–305.

22. Owens, B., Baker, W., Sumpter, D., & Cameron, K. (2016). Relational energy at work: Implications for job engagement and job performance. *Journal of Applied Psychology, 101,* 35–49.

23. Toshi Harada, personal communication with the author, 2010.

24. Examples include Haslam, S. A., Reicher, S. D., & Platow, M. J. (2020). *The new psychology of leadership: Identity, influence and power* (2nd ed.). London, England: Routledge. Also, Thomas, K. W. (2009). *Intrinsic motivation at work: Building energy and commitment* (2nd ed.). San Francisco, CA: Berrett-Koehler. Also, Pink, D. H.

(2009). *Drive: The surprising truth about what motivates us.* New York, NY: Riverhead Books.

25. Cialdini, R. B. (2008). *Influence: Science and practice.* Boston, MA: Allyn & Bacon.

26. Boyatzis, R. E., & Rochford, K. (2020). Relational climate in the workplace: Dimensions, measurement, and validation. *Frontiers in Psychology, 11,* 1–15.

27. Lauriola, M., & Iani, L. (2015). Does positivity mediate the relation of extraversion and neuroticism with subjective happiness? *PloS One, 10*(3), e0121991. https://doi.org/10.1371/journal.pone .0121991. Also, Smillie, L. D., DeYoung, C. G., & Hall, P. J. (2015). Clarifying the relation between extraversion and positive affect. *Personality, 83,* 564–574.

28. Ryan, R. M., & Deci, E. L. (2017). *Self-determination theory.* New York, NY: Guilford Press.

29. Cameron, K. S., Bright, D. S., & Caza, A. (2004). Exploring the relationships between organizational virtuousness and performance. *American Behavioral Scientist, 47,* 766–790. Also, Bright, D. S., Cameron, K. S., & Caza, A. (2006). The amplifying and buffering effects of virtuousness in downsized organizations. *Journal of Business Ethics, 64,* 249–269. Also, Cameron, K. S., Mora, C., Leutscher, T., & Calarco, C. (2011). Effects of positive practices on organizational effectiveness. *Journal of Applied Behavioral Science, 47,* 266–308.

30. Peterson, C., Park, N., Hall, N., & Seligman, M. E. P. (2009). Zest at work. *Journal of Organizational Behavior, 30,* 161–172.

Chapter 2

1. Davis, D., Lichtenwalter, R., & Chawla, N. V. (2011). Multirelational link prediction in heterogeneous information networks. In *2011 International Conference on Advances in Social Networks Analysis and Mining* (pp. 281–288).

2. Baker, W., Cross, R., & Wooten, M. (2003). Positive network analysis and energizing relationships. In K. S. Cameron, J. E. Dutton, & R. E. Quinn (Eds.), *Positive organizational scholarship* (pp. 328–342). San Francisco, CA: Berrett-Koehler. Also, Baker, W., & Dutton, J. E. (2007). Enabling positive social capital in organizations. In J. E. Dutton & B. R. Ragins (Eds.), *Exploring social relationships at work* (pp. 325–345). Mahwah, NJ: Lawrence Erlbaum. Cross, R., Baker, W. E., &

Parker, A. (2003). What creates energy in organizations? *Sloan Management Review, 44*, 51–56.

3. Burns, J. M. (1978). *Leadership*. New York, NY: Harper Collins. Also, Hogg, M. A. (2010). Influence and leadership. In S. T. Fiske, D. T. Gilbert, & G. Lindzey (Eds.), *Handbook of social psychology* (pp. 1166–1207) New York: Wiley. Also, Lunenburg, F. C. (2012). Power and leadership: An influence process. *International Journal of Management, Business, and Administration, 15*, 1–9. Also, Quinn, R. E. (2015). *The positive organization*. San Francisco, CA: Berrett-Koehler.

4. Owens, B., Baker, W., Sumpter, D., & Cameron, K. (2016). Relational energy at work: Implications for job engagement and job performance. *Journal of Applied Psychology, 101*, 35–49.

5. Fredrickson, B. L. (2009). *Positivity: Top-notch research reveals the 3-to-1 ratio that will change your life* (pp. 120–140). New York, NY: Crown Publishing.

6. Cross, R., Borgatti, S., & Parker, A. (2002). Making invisible work visible: Using social network analysis to support human networks. *California Management Review, 44*, 25–46.

7. Baker, W., Cross, R., & Wooten, M. (2003). Positive network analysis and energizing relationships. In K. S. Cameron, J. E. Dutton, & R. E. Quinn (Eds.), *Positive organizational scholarship* (pp. 328–342). San Francisco, CA: Berrett-Koehler. Also, Baker, W. B. (2000). *Through social capital: Tapping the hidden resources in your personal and business networks*. San Francisco, CA: Jossey-Bass.

8. Cross, R., Baker, W. E., & Parker, A. (2003). What creates energy in organizations? *Sloan Management Review, 44*, 51–55. Also, Baker, W., Cross, R., & Wooten, M. (2003). Positive network analysis and energizing relationships. In K. S. Cameron, J. E. Dutton, & R. E. Quinn (Eds.), *Positive organizational scholarship* (pp. 328–342). San Francisco, CA: Berrett-Koehler.

9. Baker, W. (2015, September 15). The more you energize your co-workers, the better everyone performs. *Harvard Business Review*. https://hbr.org/2016/09/the-energy-you-give-off-at-work-matters

10. Lewis, M. (2009, February 13). The no-stats all-star. *New York Times Magazine*. www.nytimes.com/2009/02/15/magazine/15Battier-t.html

11. Owens, B. P., Sumpter, D. M., Cameron, K. S., & Baker, W. E. (2018, May 28). *Relational energy and well-being*. Presented at the Cesar Ritz Well-being Conference, Brigg, Switzerland. Also, Owens, B.,

Baker, W., Sumpter, D., & Cameron, K. (2016). Relational energy at work: Implications for job engagement and job performance. *Journal of Applied Psychology, 101*, 35–49.

12. Baker, W. (2000). *Achieving success through social capital: Tapping the hidden resources in your personal and business networks.* San Francisco, CA: Jossey-Bass.

13. See rankings by *Bloomberg Business Week, Financial Times, Leadership Excellence,* and *U.S. News & World Report.*

14. Yang, Y., & Konrad, A. M. (2011). Diversity and organizational innovation: The role of employee involvement. *Journal of Organizational Behavior, 32*, 1062–1083.

15. Dobbin, F., & Kalev, A. (2016, July–August). Why diversity programs fail. *Harvard Business Review, 94*, 17–28.

Chapter 3

1. Hall, J. A. (2018). How many hours does it take to make a friend? *Journal of Social and Personal Relationships, 36*, 1278–1296.

2. Dutton, J. E. (2003). *Energize your workplace: How to build and sustain high-quality connections at work.* San Francisco, CA: Jossey-Bass. Also, Dutton, J. E., & Ragins, B. R. (Eds.) (2007). *Exploring positive relationships at work.* Mahwah, NJ: Lawrence Erlbaum. Also, Worline, M. C., Dutton, J. E., & Hardin, A. E. (2015, October 6). Forming stronger bonds with people at work. *Harvard Business Review.* https://hbr.org/2017/10/forming-stronger-bonds-with-people-at -work. Also, Heaphy, E., & Dutton, J. (2008). Positive social interactions and the human body at work: Linking organizations and physiology. *Academy of Management Review, 33*, 137–162.

3. Baker, W., Cross, R., & Wooten, M. (2003). Positive network analysis and energizing relationships. In K. S. Cameron, J. E. Dutton, & R. E. Quinn (Eds.), *Positive organizational scholarship* (pp. 328–342). San Francisco, CA: Berrett-Koehler. Baker, W., & Dutton, J. E. (2007). Enabling positive social capital in organizations. In J. E. Dutton & B. R. Ragins (Eds.), *Exploring social relationships at work* (pp. 325–345). Mahwah, NJ: Lawrence Erlbaum. Cross, R., Baker, W. E., & Parker, A. (2003). What creates energy in organizations? *Sloan Management Review, 44*, 51–56.

4. Spreitzer, G., Bacevice, P., Hendricks, H., & Garrett, P. (2021). Thriving in the *new world* of work: Implications for organizational

community. In Shani, A. N. B., & Noumair, D. A. (Eds.), *Research in organizational change and development*. New York, NY: Emerald Insight.

5. Gittell, J. H. (2016). *Transforming relationships for high performance: The power of relational coordination*. Palo Alto, CA: Stanford Business Books. Also, Gittell, J. H., Seidner, R., & Wimbush, J. (2010). A relational model of how high-performance work systems work. *Organization Science, 39*, 779–801. Also, Gittell, J. H. (2002). Coordinating mechanisms in care provider groups: Relational coordination as a mediator and input uncertainty as a moderator of performance effects. *Management Science, 48*, 1369–1389.

6. Burt, R. (1992). *Structural holes*. Cambridge, MA: Harvard Business School Press.

7. Kram, K. (1985). *Mentoring at work: Developing relationships in organizational life*. Glenview, IL: Scott Foresman.

8. Ibarra, H. (1993). Network centrality, power, and innovation involvement: Determinants of technical and administrative roles. *Academy of Management Journal, 36*, 471–501.

9. Baker, W. (2000). *Achieving success through social capital: Tapping the hidden resources in your personal and business networks*. San Francisco, CA: Jossey-Bass.

10. Ryff, C. D., & Singer, B. (Eds.). (2001). *Emotion, social relationships, and health*. Oxford, England: Oxford University Press.

11. Chapman, J. W., & Galston, W. A. (1992). *Virtue*. New York: New York University Press. Also, Comte-Sponville, A. (2001). *A small treatise of the great virtues* (C. Temerson, Trans.). New York, NY: Metropolitan Books. Also, Dent, N. (1984). *The moral psychology of the virtues*. New York, NY: Cambridge University Press. Also, MacIntyre, A. (1984). *After virtue: A study in moral theory* (2nd ed.). Notre Dame, IN: University of Notre Dame Press. Also, Weiner, N. O. (1993). *The harmony of the soul: Mental health and moral virtue reconsidered*. Albany: State University of New York Press. Also, Meyer, M. (2018) The evolution and challenges of the concept of organizational virtuousness in positive organizational scholarship. *Journal of Business Ethics, 153*, 245–264.

12. Aquinas, T. (1959). *Sentencia libri de anima* (Roberto Busa SJ, Trans.). Rome, Italy: Commissio Leonina and Vrin (Opera amnia iussu Leonis XIII, 45:1).

13. Aristotle. *Metaphysics* XII (written 350 BC). Translated by Ross, W.D., pages 3–4. Also, Sison, A. G. (2008). *Corporate governance*

and ethics: An Aristotelian perspective. Northampton, MA: Edward Elgar Publishing.

14. Demuijnck, G. (2014). Universal values and virtues in management versus cross-cultural moral relativism: An educational strategy to clear the ground for business ethics. *Journal of Business Ethics, 128*, 817–835. Also, Kinnier, R. T., Kernes, J. L., & Dautheribes, T. M. (2000). A short list of universal moral values. *Counseling and Values, 45*, 4–16.

15. Cameron, K. S., & Winn, B. (2012). Virtuousness in organizations. In K. S. Cameron & G. M. Spreitzer (Eds.), *The Oxford handbook of positive organizational scholarship* (chapter 18). New York, NY: Oxford University Press. Also, Comte-Sponville, A. (2001). *A small treatise of the great virtues* (C. Temerson, Trans.). New York, NY: Metropolitan Books. Also, Peterson, C., & Seligman, M. E. P. (2004). *Character strengths and virtues.* New York, NY: Oxford University Press.

16. Koehn, D. (2013). East meets West: Toward a universal ethic of virtue for global business. *Journal of Business Ethics, 116*, 703–715. Also, Brown, D. E. (1991). *Human universals.* New York, NY: McGraw-Hill.

17. Gouldner, A. (1960). The norm of reciprocity: A preliminary statement. *American Sociological Review, 25*, 161–179. Also, Merton, R. K. (1968). *Social organization and social structure.* New York, NY: Free Press.

18. Miller, G. F. (2007). Sexual selection for moral virtues. *The Quarterly Review of Biology, 82*, 97–125.

19. Tangney, P., Stuewig, J., & Mashek, D. (2007). Moral emotions and moral behavior. *Annual Review of Psychology, 58*, 345–372. Also, Miller, G. F. (2007). Sexual selection for moral virtues. *The Quarterly Review of Biology, 82*, 97–125. Also, see Cameron, K. S. (2012). *Positive leadership: Strategies for extraordinary performance* (chapter 1). San Francisco, CA: Berrett-Koehler.

20. Sharot, T., Riccardi, A. M., Raio, C. M., & Phelps, E. A. (2007). Neural mechanisms mediating optimism bias. *Nature, 450*, 102–106.

21. Haight, J. (2006). *The happiness hypothesis: Finding modern truth in ancient wisdom.* New York, NY: Basic Books. Also, Hauser, M. (2006). *Moral minds: How nature designed our universal sense of right and wrong.* New York, NY: ECCO. Also, Pinker, S. (1997). *How the mind works.* New York, NY: W.W. Norton.

22. Krebs, D. (1987). The challenge of altruism in biology and psychology. In C. Crawford, M. Smith, & D. Krebs (Eds.), *Sociobiology and psychology.* Hillsdale, NJ: Lawrence Erlbaum (p. 113).

23. Hamlin, J. K. (2013). Moral judgment and action in preverbal infants and toddlers: Evidence for an innate moral core. *Frontiers in Psychological Science, 22,* 186–193. https://doi.org/10.1177/09637 21412470687. Also, Hamlin, J. K., Wynn, K., Bloom, P. (2007). Social evaluation by preverbal infants. *Nature, 450,* 557–559. Also, Hamlin, J. K., & Wynn, K. (2011). Young infants prefer prosocial to antisocial others. *Cognitive Development, 26,* 30–39. Also, Sloane, S., Baillargeon, R., & Premack, D. (2012). Do infants have a sense of fairness? *Psychological Science, 23,* 196–204. Also, Warneken, F., & Tomasello, M. (2006). Altruistic helping in human infants and young chimpanzees. *Science, 311,* 1301–1303. Also, Surian, L., & Franchin, L. (2017). Toddlers selectively help fair agents. *Frontiers in Psychology, 8,* 944. doi:10.3389/fpsyg.2017.00944

24. Barragan, R. C., Brooks, R., & Meltzoff, A. N. (2020). Altruistic food sharing behavior by human infants after a hunger manipulation. *Scientific Reports, 10,* 1785. https://doi.org/10.1038/s41598-020 -58645-9

25. McCraty, R. (2016). Exploring the role of the heart in human performance: An overview of the research conducted by the Heart-Math Institute. In *Science of the Heart* (Vol. 2, pp. 53–66). Boulder Creek, CA: HeartMath Institute.

26. Cameron, K. S. (2012). *Positive leadership: Strategies for extraordinary performance.* San Francisco, CA: Berrett-Koehler.

27. Baumeister, R. F., Bratslavsky, E., Finkenauer, C., & Vohs, K. D. (2001). Bad is stronger than good. *Review of General Psychology, 5,* 323–370.

28. Wang, C. S., Galinsky, A. D., & Murnigham, J. K. (2009). Bad drives psychological reactions, but good propels behavior. *Psychological Science, 20,* 642.

29. Cameron, K. S. (2008). Paradox in positive organizational change. *Journal of Applied Behavioral Science, 44,* 7–24. Also, Cameron, K. S. (2017). Paradox in positive organizational scholarship. In M. Lewis, W. Smith, P. Jarzabkowski, & A. Langley (Eds.), *The Oxford handbook of organizational paradox* (pp. 216–238). London, England: Oxford University Press.

30. Aristotle. (1999). *Nicomachean ethics* (M. Oswald, Trans.) (pp. 1106a22–23). Upper Saddle River, NJ: Prentice Hall.

31. Cawley, M. J., Martin, J. E., & Johnson, J. A. (2000). A virtues approach to personality. *Personality and Individual Differences, 28,* 997–1013.

Chapter 4

1. Clifton, D. O., & Harter, J. K. (2003). Investing in strengths. In K. S. Cameron, J. E. Dutton, & R. E. Quinn (Eds.), *Positive organizational scholarship: Foundations of a new discipline* (pp. 111–121). San Francisco, CA: Berrett-Koehler.

2. Crocker, J., & Canevello, A. (2016). Egosystem and ecosystem: Motivational orientations of the self in relation to others. In Brown, K. W., & Leary, M. R. (Eds.), *Oxford library of psychology. The Oxford handbook of hypo-egoic phenomena* (pp. 271–283). New York, NY: Oxford University Press.

3. Brown, S. L., & Brown, R. M. (2006). Selective investment theory: Recasting the functional significance of close relationships. *Psychological Inquiry, 17,* 1–29. Brown, S. L., Nesse, R., Vinokur, A. D., & Smith, D. M. (2002). Providing support may be more beneficial than receiving it: Results from a prospective study of mortality. *Psychological Science, 14,* 320–327.

4. Schwartz, C., & Sender, R. (1991). Helping others helps oneself: Response shift effects to peer support. *Social Science and Medicine, 48,* 1563–1575.

5. Willans, A., Dunn, W., Sandstrom, G., & Madden, K. (2016). Is spending money on others good for your heart? *Health Psychology, 35*(6), 574–583. doi:10.1037/hea0000332. Also, Aknin, L. B., Broesch, T., Hamlin, J. K., & Van de Vondervoort, J. W. (2015). Prosocial behavior leads to happiness in a small-scale rural society. *Journal of Experimental Psychology: General, 144,* 788–795.

6. Okun, M. A., Yeung, E. W., & Brown, S. (2013). Volunteering by older adults and risk of mortality: A meta-analysis. *Psychology and Aging, 28*(2), 564–577.

7. Brown, S. L., Nesse, R., Vinokur, A. D., & Smith, D. M. (2002). Providing support may be more beneficial than receiving it: Results from a prospective study of mortality. *Psychological Science, 14,* 320–327.

8. Grant, A. M., Dutton, J. E., & Russo, B. D. (2008). Giving commitment: Employee support programs and the prosocial sensemaking process. *Academy of Management Journal, 51*(5), 898–918.

9. Emmons, R. A. (2007). *Thanks! How practicing gratitude can make you happier.* New York, NY: Houghton Mifflin. Also, Emmons, R. A. (2013). *Gratitude works.* New York, NY: Jossey-Bass.

10. Bonnie, K. E., & deWaal, F. B. M. (2004). Primate social reciprocity and the origin of gratitude. In R. A. Emmons & M.E. McCullough (Eds.), *The psychology of gratitude* (pp. 213–229) New York, NY: Oxford University Press.

11. McCraty, R. (2002). Influence of cardiac afferent input on heart-brain synchronization and cognitive performance. *International Journal of Psychophysiology, 45,* 72–73.

12. Tiller, W. A., McCraty, R., & Atkinson, M. (1996). Cardiac coherence: A new, noninvasive measure of autonomic nervous system order. *Alternative Therapies on Health and Medicine, 2,* 56–65.

13. Langhorst, P., Schultz, G., & Lambertz, M. (1984). Oscillating neuronal network of the common brainstem system. In K. Miyakawa, H. P. Koepchen, & C. Polosa (Eds.), *Mechanics of blood pressure waves* (pp. 257–275). Tokyo: Japan Scientific Societies Press.

14. Danner, D. D., Snowden, D. A., & Friesen, W. V. (2001). Positive emotions in early life and longevity: Findings from the nun study. *Journal of Personality and Social Psychology, 80,* 804–813. Also, Russek, L. G., & Schwartz, G. E. (1997). Feelings of parental caring predict health status in midlife: A 35-year follow-up of the Harvard Mastery of Stress study. *Journal of Behavioral Medicine, 20,* 1–13.

15. Isen, A. M. (1987). Positive affect, cognitive processes, and social behavior. *Advances in Experimental Social Psychology, 20,* 203–253. Also, Isen, A. M., Daubman, K. A., & Nowicki, G. P. (1987). Positive affect facilitates creative problem solving. *Journal of Personality and Social Psychology, 52,* 1122–1131.

16. Redwine, L. S., Henry, B. L., Pung, M. A., Wilson, K., Chinh, K., Knight, B., . . . Mills, P.J., (2018). Pilot randomized study of a gratitude journaling intervention on heart rate variability and inflammatory biomarkers in patients with Stage B heart failure. *Psychosomatic Medicine, 78,* 667–676. doi:10.1097/PSY.0000000000000316

17. Emmons, R. A. (2007). *Thanks! How practicing gratitude can make you happier.* New York, NY: Houghton Mifflin. Also, Emmons, R. A. (2003). Acts of gratitude in organizations. In K. S. Cameron, J. E. Dutton, & R. E. Quinn (Eds.), *Positive organizational scholarship* (pp. 81–93). San Francisco, CA: Berrett-Koehler.

18. Kini, P., Wong, J., McInnis, S., Gabana, N., & Brown, J. W. (2016). The effects of gratitude expression on neural activity. *Neuro-*

Image, 128, 1–10. Also, Wong, Y. J., Owen, J., Gabana, N. T., Brown, J. W., McInnis, S., Toth, P., & Gilman, L. (2018). Does gratitude writing improve the mental health of psychotherapy clients? Evidence from a randomized controlled trial. *Psychotherapy Research, 28,* 192–202. doi:10.1080/10503307.2016.1169332

19. Cameron, K. S., Bright, D., & Caza, A. (2004). Exploring the relationships between organizational virtuousness and performance. *American Behavioral Scientist, 47,* 766–779. Also, Cameron, K. S., & Caza, A. (2002). Organizational and leadership virtues and the role of forgiveness. *Journal of Leadership and Organizational Studies, 9,* 33–48.

20. Bright, D. S., Cameron, K. S., & Caza, A. (2006). The amplifying and buffering effects of virtuousness in downsized organizations. *Journal of Business Ethics, 64,* 249–269. Also, Gittell, J. H., Cameron, K. S., Lim, S., & Rivas, V. (2006). Relationships, layoffs, and organizational resilience. *Journal of Applied Behavioral Science, 42,* 300–328.

21. Owens, B. P., Rowatt, W. C., & Wilkins, A. L. (2012). Exploring the relevance and implications of humility in organizations. In K. S. Cameron & G. M. Spreitzer (Eds.), *The Oxford handbook of positive organizational scholarship* (pp. 260–272). New York, NY: Oxford University Press.

22. Ou, A. Y., Tsui, A. S., Kinicki, A., Waldman, D., Song, L. J., & Xiao, Z. X. (2014). Understanding humble chief executive officers: Connections to top management team integration and middle manager responses. *Administrative Science Quarterly, 59,* 34–72.

23. Owens, B., & Hekman, D. (2012). Modeling how to grow: An inductive examination of humble leader behaviors, contingencies, and outcomes. *Academy of Management Journal, 55,* 787–818. Also, Owens, B., Johnson, M., & Mitchell, T. (2013). Expressed humility in organizations: Implications for performance, teams, and leadership. *Organization Science, 24,* 1517–1538. Also, Owens, B. P., Rowatt, W. C., & Wilkins, A. L. (2011). Exploring the relevance and implications of humility in organizations. In K. S. Cameron & G. M. Spreitzer (Eds.), *The Oxford handbook of positive organizational scholarship* (pp. 260–272). New York, NY: Oxford University Press.

24. Vera, D., & Rodriguez-Lopez, A. (2004). Humility as a source of competitive advantage. *Organizational Dynamics, 33,* 393–408. Also, Collins, J. (2001). *Good to great.* New York, NY: Harper Collins.

25. McCraty, R., & Childre, D. (2004). The grateful heart: The psychophysiology of appreciation. In R. A. Emmons & M. E. McCullough (Eds.), *The psychology of gratitude* (pp. 230–255). New York, NY: Oxford University Press.

26. Kramer, R. M. (1999). Trust and distrust in organizations: Emerging perspectives, enduring questions. *Annual Review of Psychology, 50*, 569–598. Also, Kramer, R. M., & Tyler, T. R. (2004). *Trust in organizations*. Thousand Oaks, CA: Sage.

27. Mishra, A. K., & Mishra, K. E. (2013). *Becoming a trustworthy leader*. New York, NY: Routledge.

28. Rothschild, N. (2020, March 24). Sweden is open for business during its coronavirus outbreak: The Scandinavian country believes its distinctive high-trust culture will protect it from needing to shut down for the pandemic. *Foreign Policy*. https://foreignpolicy.com/2020/03/24/sweden-coronavirus-open-for-business

29. Edelman. (2018). Edelman Trust Barometer. https://www.edelman.com/trustbarometer. Also, Mishra, A. K., & Mishra, K. E. (2013). *Becoming a trustworthy leader*. New York, NY: Routledge.

30. Bernath, M. S., & Feshbach, N. D. (1995). Children's trust: Theory, assessment, development, and research implications. *Applied Preventative Psychology, 4*, 1–19. Also, Lewicki, R. J., Wierthoff, C., & Tomlinson, E. C. (2005). What is the role of trust in organizational justice? In J. Greenberg & J. A. Colquitt (Eds.), *Handbook of organizational justice* (pp. 247–270). Mahwah, NJ: Lawrence Erlbaum. Also, Rowe, R., & Calnan, M. (2006). Trust relations in health care: Developing a theoretical framework from the new NHS. *Journal of Health Organization and Management, 20*, 376–396.

31. Erickson, E. H. (2008a). *Gioventu e crisi d' identita*. Rome, Italy: Armando. Also, Erickson, E. H. (2008b). *Infanzia e societa*. Rome, Italy: Armando.

32. Małgorzata Szcześniak, M., Colaço, M., & Rondón, G. (2012). Development of interpersonal trust among children and adolescents. *Polish Psychological Bulletin, 43*, 50–58.

33. Mishra, A. K., & Mishra, K. E. (2013). *Becoming a trustworthy leader*. New York, NY: Routledge. Also, Mishra, A. K., & Spreitzer, G. M. (1998). Explaining how survivors respond to downsizing: The roles of trust, empowerment, justice, and work design. *Academy of Management Review, 23*, 567–588. Also, Fukuyama, F. (1995). *Trust: The social virtues of the creation of prosperity*. New York, NY: Free Press. Also, Brockner, J., Siegel, P. A., Daly, J. P., & Tyler, T. (1997).

When trust matters: The moderating effects of outcome favorability. *Administrative Science Quarterly, 43,* 558–583. Also, Malhotra, D., & Lumineau, F. (2011). Trust and collaboration in the aftermath of conflict. *Academy of Management Journal, 54,* 981–998. Also, Colquitt, J. A., Scott, B. A., & LePine, J. A. (2007). Trust, trustworthiness, and trust propensity: A meta-analytic test of their unique relationships with risk taking and job performance. *Journal of Applied Psychology, 92,* 909–927. Also, Szulanski, G., Cappette, R., & Jensen, R. J. (2004). When and how trustworthiness matters. *Organizational Science, 15,* 600–613.

34. Gittell, J. H., Cameron, K. S., Lim, S., & Rivas, V. (2006). Relationships, layoffs, and organizational resilience. *Journal of Applied Behavioral Science, 42,* 300–328.

35. Covey, S. R. (2004). *Seven habits of highly effective people.* New York, NY: Simon and Schuster.

36. Cameron, K. S. (2020). Building relationships by communicating supportively. In D. A. Whetten & K. S. Cameron (Eds.), *Developing management skills* (10th ed., pp. 188–224). Pearson Education.

Chapter 5

1. For additional examples, see Cameron, K. S. (2012). *Positive leadership: Strategies for extraordinary performance.* San Francisco, CA: Berrett-Koehler. Also, Cameron, K. S. (2013). *Practicing positive leadership.* San Francisco, CA: Berrett-Koehler.

2. Benito, A., Srinivasan, B., Yadav, P., Majithia, M., and Abraham, N. (2019). Improving learning in higher education: Case study of the effects of positive leadership on students and faculty. *International Journal of Arts and Social Science, 2.* 36–45. Also, Benito, A., Jiménez-Bernal, M., Lajud-Desentis, C., Moreno-Melgarejo, C., & Muñoz-Sepulveda, J. (2019). Expanding the limits of positive leadership into the world of higher education. *International Journal of Learning, Teaching and Educational Research, 18*(2), 29–42.

3. The information regarding STC and Biyari was obtained from personal interviews with Biyari and six senior executives in STC, along with five lower-level employees, on January 7, 2019, in Riyadh, Saudi Arabia.

4. Taken from Cameron, K. S. (2012). *Positive leadership: Strategies for extraordinary performance.* San Francisco, CA: Berrett-Koehler.

5. Video speech in the summer of 2020 by Kevin Hegarty upon the completion of the 90-in-90 Challenge. The video was distributed to all B&F employees.

6. Cameron, K. S., Dutton, J. E., & Quinn, R. E. (2003). *Positive organizational scholarship*. San Francisco, CA: Berrett-Koehler. Also, Cameron, K. S. (2013). *Practicing positive leadership*. San Francisco, CA: Berrett-Koehler. Also, Cameron, K. S., & Lavine, M. (2006). *Making the impossible possible: Leading extraordinary performance— the Rocky Flats Story*. San Francisco, CA: Berrett-Koehler.

7. Cooperrider, D. L. (2008). *The appreciative inquiry handbook: For leaders of change*. San Francisco, CA: Berrett-Koehler.

Chapter 6

1. Ehrenreich, B. (2009). *Bright-sided: How positive thinking is undermining America*. New York, NY: Henry Holt. Also, Fineman, S. (2006). On being positive: Concerns and counterpoints. *Academy of Management Review, 31*(2), 270–291. Also, George, J. M. (2004). Book review of positive organizational scholarship: Foundations of a new discipline. *Administrative Science Quarterly, 49,* 325–330. Also, Hackman, J. R. (2008). The perils of positivity. *Journal of Organizational Behavior, 30,* 309–319.

2. Diener, E. (2009). *The collected work of Ed Diener—the science of well-being, culture and well-being, and assessing well-being*. New York, NY: Springer. Also, Diener, E., & Chan, M. Y. (2010). Happy people live longer: Subjective well-being contributes to health and longevity. *Applied Psychology: Health and Well-Being, 3, 1–43*. Retrieved from SSRN. https://ssrn.com/abstract=1701957. Also, Fredrickson, B. L. (2009). *Positivity: Top-notch research reveals the 3-to-1 ratio that will change your life*. New York, NY: Crown Publishing. Also, Pressman, S. D., & Cohen, S. (2005). Does positive affect influence health? *Psychological Bulletin, 131,* 925–971.

3. Diener, E., Pressman, S., Hunter, J., & Chase, D. (2017). If, why, and when subjective well-being influences health, and future needed research. *Applied Psychology: Health and Well-Being, 9,* 133–167. Also, Tenny, E. R., Poole, J. M., & Diener, E. (2016). Does positivity enhance work performance? Why, when, and what we don't know. *Research in Organizational Behavior, 36,* 27–46.

4. Cameron, K. S., Mora, C. E., Leutscher, T., & Calarco, M. (2011). Effects of positive practices on organizational effectiveness. *Journal*

of Applied Behavioral Science, 47, 1–43. Also, Cameron, K. S., Bright, D., & Caza, A. (2004). Exploring the relationships between organizational virtuousness and performance. *American Behavioral Scientist, 47,* 766–790. Also, Bright, D. S., Cameron, K. S., & Caza, A. (2006). The amplifying and buffering effects of virtuousness in downsized organizations. *Journal of Business Ethics, 64,* 249–269. Also, Gittell, J. H., Cameron, K. S., Lim, S., & Rivas, V. (2006). Relationships, layoffs, and organizational resilience. *Journal of Applied Behavioral Science, 42,* 300–328.

5. James, W. (1902). *The varieties of religious experience: A study in human nature.* Cambridge, MA: Harvard University Press.

6. Allport, G. W. (1960). *Becoming: Basic considerations for a psychology of personality.* New Haven, CT: Yale University Press.

7. Jahoda, M. (1959). *Current concepts of positive mental health.* New York, NY: Basic Books.

8. Maslow, A. H. (1968). *Toward a psychology of being.* New York, NY: Van Nostrand.

9. McGregor, D. (1960). *The human side of enterprise.* New York, NY: McGraw-Hill.

10. Bennis, W. (1963). New role for the behavioral sciences: Effecting organizational change. *Administrative Science Quarterly, 8*(2), 125–165.

11. Sharot, T., Riccardi, A. M., Raio, C. M., & Phelps, E. A. (2007). Neural mechanisms mediating optimism bias. *Nature, 450,* 102–106.

12. McCraty, R., & Childre, D. (2004). The grateful heart. In R. A. Emmons & M. E. McCullough (Eds.), *The psychology of gratitude* (pp. 230–255). New York, NY: Oxford University Press.

13. Kok, B. E., Cohen, M. A., Catalino, L. I., Vacharlksemsuk, T., Algoe, S. B., Brantley, M., & Fredrickson, B. M. (2013). How positive emotions build physical health: Perceived positive social connections account for the upward spiral between emotions and vagal tone. *Psychological Science, 24,* 1123–1132.

14. McCraty, R. (2016). Exploring the role of the heart in human performance: An overview of the research conducted by the HeartMath Institute. In *Science of the Heart* (Vol. 2, pp. 53–66). Boulder Creek, CA: HeartMath Institute.

15. Cameron, K. S., & Lavine, M. (2006). *Making the impossible possible: Leading extraordinary performance—the Rocky Flats story.* San Francisco, CA: Berrett-Koehler. Also, Cameron, K. S., Mora, C. E.,

Leutscher, T., & Calarco, M. (2011). Effects of positive practices on organizational effectiveness. *Journal of Applied Behavioral Science, 47,* 1–43. Also, Cameron, K. S., Bright, D., & Caza, A. (2004). Exploring the relationships between organizational virtuousness and performance. *American Behavioral Scientist, 47,* 766–790. Also, Bright, D. S., Cameron, K. S., & Caza, A. (2006). The amplifying and buffering effects of virtuousness in downsized organizations. *Journal of Business Ethics, 64,* 249–269.

16. Cascio, W. F. (2003). Changes in workers, work, and organizations. In W. C. Borman, D. R. Ilgen, & R. J. Klimoski (Eds.), *Handbook of psychology: Industrial and organizational psychology, Vol. 12* (pp. 401–422). John Wiley & Sons Inc.

17. For example, Cameron, K. S., & Spreitzer, G. M. (2012). *The Oxford handbook of positive organizational scholarship.* New York, NY: Oxford University Press. Also, Seppala, E. C. (2017). *The happiness track: How to apply the science of happiness to accelerate your success.* New York, NY: Harper Collins. Also, David, S. A., Boniwell, I., & Ayers, A. C. (2013). *The Oxford handbook of happiness.* New York, NY: Oxford University Press. Also, Seppala, E. C., Simon-Thomas, E., Brown, S. L., Worline, M. C., Cameron, D., & Doty, J. R. (2017). *The Oxford handbook of compassion science.* New York, NY: Oxford University Press.

18. For example, Cameron, K. S. (2021). Applications of positive organizational scholarship in institutions of higher education. In Kern, M., & Wehmeyer, M. L. (Eds.), *Palgrave handbook of positive education* (chapter 27). New York, NY: Palgrave Macmillan.

19. Weick, K. (1984). Small wins: Redefining the scale of social problems. *American Psychologist, 39:* 4049.

20. Zak, P. J. (2017, January–February). The neuroscience of trust. *Harvard Business Review,* pp. 84–90.

21. Wong, P. T. P., & Roy, S. (2018). Critique of positive psychology and positive interventions. In N. J. L. Brown, T. Lomas, & F. J. Eiroa-Orosa (Eds.), *The Routledge international handbook of critical positive psychology* (pp. 142–160). London: Routledge/Taylor & Francis Group. Also, Held, B. S. (2004). The negative side of positive psychology. *Journal of Humanistic Psychology, 44,* 9–46. Also, Smith, J. (2019, November 20). Is positive psychology all it's cracked up to be? *Vox.* https://www.vox.com/the-highlight/2019/11/13/20955328/. Also, Van Nuys, D. (November 3, 2010). Popping the happiness bubble:

The backlash against positive psychology. *Psychology Today.* www .psychologytoday.com/us/blog/the-happiness-dispatch/201011/

22. Hepach, R., & Warneken, F. (2018). Editorial review: Early development of prosocial behaviour: Revealing the foundation of human prosociality. *Current Opinion in Psychology, 20,* iv–vii. Also, Roth-Hanania, R., Davidov, M., & Zahn-Waxler, C. (2011). Empathy development from 8 to 16 months: Early signs of concern for others. *Infant Behavior and Development, 34,* 447–458. Also, Van de Vondervoort, J., & Hamlin, J. K. (2018). The early emergence of sociomoral evaluation: Infants prefer prosocial others. *Current Opinion in Psychology, 20,* 77–81.

23. Baumeister, R. F., Bratslavsky, E., Finkenauer, C., & Vohs, K. D. (2001). Bad is stronger than good. *Review of General Psychology, 5,* 323–370.

☀ REFERENCES

Abramowitz, J. A., Tolin, D. F., & Street, G. P. (2001). Paradoxical effects of thought suppression: A meta-analysis of controlled studies. *Clinical Psychology Review, 21,* 683–703.

Akin, L. B., Broesch, T., Hamlin, J. K., & Van de Vondervoort, J. W. (2015). Prosocial behavior leads to happiness in a small-scale rural society. *Journal of Experimental Psychology: General, 144,* 788–795.

Allport, G. W. (1960). *Becoming: Basic considerations for a psychology of personality.* New Haven, CT: Yale University Press.

Aneja, S. (2014). *Happiology: The science of creating your happiness.* Denver, CO: Outskirts Press.

Aquinas, T. (1959). *Sentencia libri de anima* (Roberto Busa SJ, Trans.). Rome, Italy: Commissio Leonina and Vrin (Opera amnia iussu Leonis XIII, 45:1).

Aristotle. (1999). *Nicomachean ethics.* (M. Oswald, Trans.). Upper Saddle River, NJ: Prentice Hall.

Aristotle. *Metaphysics* XII (written 350 BC). Translated by Ross, W. D., pp. 3–4.

Baker, W. (2000). *Achieving success through social capital: Tapping the hidden resources in your personal and business networks.* San Francisco, CA: Jossey-Bass.

Baker, W. (2015, September 15). The more you energize your coworkers, the better everyone performs. *Harvard Business Review.* https://hbr.org/2016/09/the-energy-you-give-off-at-work -matters

Baker, W. (2019). Emotional energy, relational energy, and organizational energy: Toward a multilevel model. *Annual Review of Organizational Psychology and Organizational Behavior, 6,* 373–395.

Baker, W., Cross, R., & Wooten, M. (2003). Positive network analysis and energizing relationships. In K. S. Cameron, J. E. Dutton, & R. E. Quinn (Eds.), *Positive organizational scholarship* (pp. 328–342). San Francisco, CA: Berrett-Koehler.

Baker, W., & Dutton, J. E. (2007). Enabling positive social capital in organizations. In J. E. Dutton &B. R. Ragins (Eds.), *Exploring social relationships at work* (pp. 325–345). Mahwah, NJ: Lawrence Erlbaum.

Barragan, R. C., Brooks, R., & Meltzoff, A. N. (2020). Altruistic food sharing behavior by human infants after a hunger manipulation. *Scientific Reports, 10,* 1785. https://doi.org/10.1038/s41598-020-58645-9

Baumeister, R. F., Bratslavsky, E., Finkenauer, C., & Vohs, K. D. (2001). Bad is stronger than good. *Review of General Psychology, 5,* 323–370.

Beck, R., & Harter, J. (2015). Managers account for 70% of variance in employee engagement. *Gallup Business Journal.* https://news.gallup.com/businessjournal/182792/managers-account-variance-employee-engagement.aspx

Benito, A., Srinivasan, B., Yadav, P., Majithia, M., and Abraham, N. (2019). Improving learning in higher education: Case study of the effects of positive leadership on students and faculty. *International Journal of Arts and Social Science, 2,* 36–45.

Benito, A., Jiménez-Bernal, M., Lajud-Desentis, C., Moreno-Melgarejo, C., & Muñoz-Sepulveda, J. (2019). Expanding the limits of positive leadership into the world of higher education. *International Journal of Learning, Teaching and Educational Research, 18*(2), 29–42.

Bennis, W. (1963). New role for the behavioral sciences: Effecting organizational change. *Administrative Science Quarterly, 8*(2), 125–165.

Bernath, M. S., & Feshbach, N. D. (1995). Children's trust: Theory, assessment, development, and research implications. *Applied Preventative Psychology, 4,* 1–19.

Bonnie, K. E., & deWaal, F. B. M. (2004). Primate social reciprocity and the origin of gratitude. In R. A. Emmons & M. E. McCullough (Eds.), *The psychology of gratitude* (pp. 213–229). New York, NY: Oxford University Press.

Boyatzis, R. E., & Rochford, K. (2020). Relational climate in the workplace: Dimensions, measurement, and validation. *Frontiers in Psychology, 11,* 1–15.

Bright, D. S., Cameron, K. S., & Caza, A. (2006). The amplifying and buffering effects of virtuousness in downsized organizations. *Journal of Business Ethics, 64,* 249–269.

Brockner, J., Siegel, P. A., Daly, J. P., & Tyler, T. (1997). When trust matters: The moderating effects of outcome favorability. *Administrative Science Quarterly, 43,* 558–583.

Brown, C. G. (1999). *The energy of life: The science of what makes our minds and bodies work.* New York, NY: Free Press.

Brown, D. E. (1991). *Human universals.* New York, NY: McGraw-Hill.

Brown, S. L., & Brown, R. M. (2006). Selective investment theory: Recasting the functional significance of close relationships. *Psychological Inquiry, 17,* 1–29.

Brown, S. L., Nesse, R., Vinokur, A. D., & Smith, D. M. (2002). Providing support may be more beneficial than receiving it: Results from a prospective study of mortality. *Psychological Science, 14,* 320–327.

Burns, J. M. (1978). *Leadership.* New York, NY: Harper Collins.

Burt, R. (1992). *Structural holes.* Cambridge, MA: Harvard Business School Press.

Cameron, K. S. (2008). Paradox in positive organizational change. *Journal of Applied Behavioral Science, 44,* 7–24.

Cameron, K. S. (2012). *Positive leadership: Strategies for extraordinary performance.* San Francisco, CA: Berrett-Koehler.

Cameron, K. S. (2013). *Practicing positive leadership.* San Francisco, CA: Berrett-Koehler.

Cameron, K. S. (2017). Paradox in positive organizational scholarship. In M. Lewis, W. Smith, P. Jarzabkowski, and A. Langley (Eds.), *The Oxford handbook of organizational paradox* (pp. 216–238). London, England: Oxford University Press.

Cameron, K. S. (2020). Building relationships by communicating supportively. In D. A. Whetten and K. S. Cameron (Eds.), *Developing management skills* (10th ed., pp. 188–224). Pearson Education.

Cameron, K. S. (2021). Applications of positive organizational scholarship in institutions of higher education. In Kern, M., & Wehmeyer, M. L., (Eds.), *Palgrave handbook of positive education* (chapter 27). New York, NY: Palgrave Macmillan.

Cameron, K. S., Bright, D. S., & Caza, A. (2004). Exploring the relationships between organizational virtuousness and performance. *American Behavioral Scientist, 47,* 766–790.

Cameron, K. S., & Caza, A. (2002). Organizational and leadership virtues and the role of forgiveness. *Journal of Leadership and Organizational Studies, 9,* 33–48.

Cameron, K. S., Dutton, J. E., & Quinn, R. E. (2003). *Positive organizational scholarship.* San Francisco, CA: Berrett-Koehler.

Cameron, K. S., & Lavine, M. (2006). *Making the impossible possible: Leading extraordinary performance—the Rocky Flats story.* San Francisco, CA: Berrett-Koehler.

Cameron, K. S., Mora, C. E., Leutscher, T., & Calarco, M. (2011). Effects of positive practices on organizational effectiveness. *Journal of Applied Behavioral Science, 47,* 266–308.

Cameron, K. S., & Spreitzer, G. M. (2012). *The Oxford handbook of positive organizational scholarship.* New York, NY: Oxford University Press.

Cameron, K. S., & Winn, B. (2012). Virtuousness in organizations. In K. S. Cameron & G. M. Spreitzer (Eds.), *The Oxford handbook of positive organizational scholarship.* New York, NY: Oxford University Press.

Cascio, W. F. (2003). Changes in workers, work, and organizations. In W. C. Borman, D. R. Ilgen, & R. J. Klimoski (Eds.), *Handbook of psychology: Industrial and organizational psychology, Vol. 12* (pp. 401–422). John Wiley & Sons Inc. https://doi.org/10.1002/0471264385.wei1216

Cawley, M. J., Martin, J. E., & Johnson, J. A. (2000). A virtues approach to personality. *Personality and Individual Differences, 28,* 997–1013.

Chapman, J. W., & Galston, W. A. (1992). *Virtue*. New York: New York University Press.

Christoforou, P. S., & Ashforth, B. E. (2014). Revisiting the debate on the relationship between display rules and performance: Considering the explicitness of display rules. *Journal of Applied Psychology, 100*, 249–261.

Cialdini, R. B. (2008). *Influence: Science and Practice*. Boston, MA: Allyn & Bacon.

Clifton, D. O., & Harter, J. K. (2003). Investing in strengths. In K. S. Cameron, J. E. Dutton, and R. E. Quinn (Eds.), *Positive organizational scholarship: Foundations of a new discipline* (pp. 111–121). San Francisco, CA: Berrett-Koehler.

Cole, M. S., Bruch, H., & Vogel, B. (2011). Energy at work: A measurement validation and linkage to unit effectiveness. *Journal of Organizational Behavior, 33*, 445–467.

Collins, J. (2001). *Good to great*. New York, NY: Harper Collins.

Colquitt, J. A., Scott, B. A., & LePine, J. A. (2007). Trust, trustworthiness, and trust propensity: A meta-analytic test of their unique relationships with risk taking and job performance. *Journal of Applied Psychology, 92*, 909–927.

Comte-Sponville, A. (2001). *A small treatise of the great virtues* (C. Temerson, Trans.). New York, NY: Metropolitan Books.

Cooperrider, D. L. (2008). *The appreciative inquiry handbook: For leaders of change*. San Francisco, CA: Berrett-Koehler.

Covey, S. R. (2004). *Seven habits of highly effective people*. New York, NY: Simon and Schuster.

Crocker, J., & Canevello, A. (2016). Egosystem and ecosystem: Motivational orientations of the self in relation to others. In Brown, K. W., & Leary, M. R. (Eds.), *Oxford library of psychology. The Oxford handbook of hypo-egoic phenomena* (pp. 271–283). New York, NY: Oxford University Press.

Cross, R., Baker, W. E., & Parker, A. (2003). What creates energy in organizations? *Sloan Management Review, 44*, 51–56.

D'Amato, M. R., & Jagoda, H. (1962). Effect of early exposure to photic stimulation on brightness discrimination and exploratory behavior. *Journal of Genetic Psychology, 101*, 267ff.

Danner, D. D., Snowden, D. A., & Friesen, W. V. (2001). Positive emotions in early life and longevity: Findings from the nun study. *Journal of Personality and Social Psychology, 80,* 804–813.

David, S. A., Boniwell, I., & Ayers, A. C. (2013). *The Oxford handbook of happiness.* New York, NY: Oxford University Press.

Davis, D., Lichtenwalter, R., & Chawla, N. V. (2011). Multi-relational link prediction in heterogeneous information networks. In *2011 International Conference on Advances in Social Networks Analysis and Mining* (pp. 281–288).

Demuijnck, G. (2014). Universal values and virtues in management versus cross-cultural moral relativism: An educational strategy to clear the ground for business ethics. *Journal of Business Ethics, 128,* 817–835.

Dent, N. (1984). *The moral psychology of the virtues.* New York, NY: Cambridge University Press.

Diener, E. (2009). *The collected work of Ed Diener—the science of well-being, culture and well-being, and assessing well-being.* New York, NY: Springer.

Diener, E., & Chan, M. Y. (2010, November 23). Happy people live longer: Subjective well-being contributes to health and longevity. *Applied Psychology: Health and Well-Being, 3,* 1–43. Retrieved from SSRN. https://ssrn.com/abstract=1701957

Diener, E., Pressman, S., Hunter, J., & Chase, D. (2017). If, why, and when subjective well-being influences health, and future needed research. *Applied Psychology: Health and Well-Being, 9,* 133–167.

Dobbin, F., & Kalev, A. (2016, July–August). Why diversity programs fail. *Harvard Business Review.*

Doidge, N. (2016). *The brain's way of healing.* New York, NY: Penguin Books.

Dutton, J. E. (2003). *Energize your workplace: How to build and sustain high-quality connections at work.* San Francisco, CA: Jossey-Bass Publishers.

Dutton, J. E., & Ragins, B. R. (Eds.). (2007). *Exploring positive relationships at work.* Mahwah, NJ: Lawrence Erlbaum.

Edelman. (2018). Edelman Trust Barometer. https://www.edelman.com/trustbarometer

Ehrenreich, B. (2009). *Bright-sided: How positive thinking is undermining America.* New York, NY: Henry Holt.

Einstein, A. (1905). Concerning an heuristic point of view toward the emission and transformation of light. *Annalen der Physik, 17*, 132–148.

Emmons, R. A. (2003). Acts of gratitude in organizations. In K. S. Cameron, J. E. Dutton, & R. E. Quinn (Eds.), *Positive organizational scholarship* (pp. 81–93). San Francisco, CA: Berrett-Koehler.

Emmons, R. A., (2007). *Thanks! How practicing gratitude can make you happier.* New York, NY: Houghton Mifflin.

Emmons, R. A. (2013) *Gratitude works.* New York, NY: Jossey-Bass.

Erhard-Seibold, E. V. (1937). The heliotrope tradition. *Orisis, 3,* 22–46.

Erickson, E. H. (2008a). *Gioventu e crisi d' identita.* Rome, Italy: Armando.

Erickson, E. H. (2008b). *Infanzia e societa.* Rome, Italy: Armando.

Fineman, S. (2006). On being positive: Concerns and counterpoints. *Academy of Management Review, 31*(2), 270–291.

Frantz, T. T., Trolley, B. C., & Farrell, M. M. (1998). Positive aspects of grief. *Pastoral Psychology, 47,* 3–17.

Fredrickson, B. L. (2009). *Positivity: Top-notch research reveals the 3-to-1 ratio that will change your life.* New York, NY: Crown Publishing.

Fukuyama, F. (1995). *Trust: The social virtues of the creation of prosperity.* New York, NY: Free Press.

George, J. M. (2004). Book review of positive organizational scholarship: Foundations of a new discipline. *Administrative Science Quarterly, 49,* 325–330.

Gittell, J. H. (2002). Coordinating mechanisms in care provider groups: Relational coordination as a mediator and input uncertainty as a moderator of performance effects. *Management Science, 48,* 1369–1389.

Gittell, J. H. (2016). *Transforming relationships for high performance: The power of relational coordination.* Palo Alto, CA: Stanford Business Books.

Gittell, J. H., Cameron, K. S., Lim, S., & Rivas, V. (2006). Relationships, layoffs, and organizational resilience. *Journal of Applied Behavioral Science, 42,* 300–328.

Gittell, J. H., Seidner, R., & Wimbush, J. (2010). A relational model of how high-performance work systems work. *Organization Science, 39,* 779–801.

Gouldner, A. (1960). The norm of reciprocity: A preliminary statement. *American Sociological Review, 25,* 161–179.

Grandey, A., Foo, S. C., Groth, M., & Goodwin, R. E. (2012). Free to be you and me: A climate of authenticity alleviates burnout from emotional labor. *Journal of Occupational Health Psychology, 17,* 1–14.

Grant, A. M., Dutton, J. E., & Russo, B. D. (2008). Giving commitment: Employee support programs and the prosocial sensemaking process. *Academy of Management Journal, 51*(5), 898–918.

Gyory, H. (2008). Medicine in ancient Egypt. In H. Selin (Ed.), *Encyclopedia of the history of science, technology, and medicine in non-Western cultures* (2nd ed., pp. 1508–1518). New York, NY: Springer.

Hackman, J. R. (2008). The perils of positivity. *Journal of Organizational Behavior, 30,* 309–319.

Haight, J. (2006). *The happiness hypothesis: Finding modern truth in ancient wisdom.* New York, NY: Basic Books.

Hall, J. A. (2018). How many hours does it take to make a friend? *Journal of Social and Personal Relationships, 36,* 1278–1296.

Hamblin, M. R. (2017). Ultraviolet irradiation of blood: "The cure that time forgot?" *Advanced Experimental Medical Biology, 996,* 295–309.

Hamblin, M. R. (2018). Photobiomodulation for traumatic brain injury and stroke. *Journal of Neuroscience Research, 96*(4), 731–743.

Hamlin, J. K. (2013). Moral judgment and action in preverbal infants and toddlers: Evidence for an innate moral core. *Frontiers in Psychological Science, 22,* 186–193. https://doi.org/10.1177/0963721412470687

Hamlin, J. K., & Wynn, K. (2011). Young infants prefer prosocial to antisocial others. *Cognitive Development, 26,* 30–39.

Hamlin, J. K., Wynn, K., & Bloom, P. (2007). Social evaluation by preverbal infants. *Nature, 450,* 557–559.

Haslam, S. A., Reicher, S. D., & Platow, M. J. (2020). *The new psychology of leadership: Identity, influence and power* (2nd ed.). London, England: Routledge.

Hauser, M. (2006). *Moral minds: How nature designed our universal sense of right and wrong.* New York, NY: ECCO.

Heaphy, E., & Dutton, J. (2008). Positive social interactions and the human body at work: Linking organizations and physiology. *Academy of Management Review, 33,* 137–162.

Held, B. S. (2004). The negative side of positive psychology. *Journal of Humanistic Psychology, 44,* 9–46.

Hepach, R., & Warneken, F. (2018). Editorial review: Early development of prosocial behaviour: Revealing the foundation of human prosociality. *Current Opinion in Psychology, 20,* iv–vii.

Hogg, M. A. (2010). Influence and leadership. In S. T. Fiske, D. T. Gilbert, & G. Lindzey (Eds.), *Handbook of social psychology* (pp. 1166–1207). New York, NY: Wiley.

Ibarra, H. (1993). Network centrality, power, and innovation involvement: Determinants of technical and administrative roles. *Academy of Management Journal, 36,* 471–501.

Isen, A. M. (1987). Positive affect, cognitive processes, and social behavior. *Advances in Experimental Social Psychology, 20,* 203–253.

Isen, A. M., Daubman, K. A., & Nowicki, G. P. (1987). Positive affect facilitates creative problem solving. *Journal of Personality and Social Psychology, 52,* 1122–1131.

Isobe, Y., & Nishino, H. (2004). Signal transmission from the suprachiasmatic nucleus to the pineal gland via the paraventricular nucleus: Analyzed from arg-vasopressin peptide, rPer2mRNA and AVPmRNA changes in pineal AA-NATmRNA after melatonin injection during light and dark periods. *Brain Research, 1013,* 204–211.

Jahoda, M. (1959). *Current concepts of positive mental health.* New York, NY: Basic Books.

James, W. (1902). *The varieties of religious experience: A study in human nature.* Cambridge, MA: Harvard University Press.

Johnston, E. S. (1931). Phototropism. In Abbot, C. G. (Ed.), *Smithsonian Scientific Series* (Vol. 11). New York, NY: Smithsonian Institution Series.

Kini, P., Wong, J., McInnis, S., Gabana, N., & Brown, J. W. (2016). The effects of gratitude expression on neural activity. *Neuro-Image, 128,* 1–10.

Kinnier, R. T., Kernes, J. L., & Dautheribes, T. M. (2000). A short list of universal moral values. *Counseling and Values, 45,* 4–16.

Koehn, D. (2013). East meets West: Toward a universal ethic of virtue for global business. *Journal of Business Ethics, 116,* 703–715.

Kok, B. E., Cohen, M. A., Catalino, L. I., Vacharlksemsuk, T., Algoe, S. B., Brantley, M., & Fredrickson, B. M. (2013). How positive emotions build physical health: Perceived positive social connections account for the upward spiral between emotions and vagal tone. *Psychological Science, 24,* 1123–1132.

Konnikova, M. (2016, July 30). What makes people feel upbeat at work. *The New Yorker.* https://www.newyorker.com/science/maria-konnikova/what-makes-people-feel-upbeat-at-work

Kram, K. (1985). *Mentoring at work: Developing relationships in organizational life.* Glenview, IL: Scott Foresman.

Kramer, R. M. (1999). Trust and distrust in organizations: Emerging perspectives, enduring questions. *Annual Review of Psychology, 50,* 569–598.

Kramer, R. M., & Tyler, T. R. (2004). *Trust in organizations.* Thousand Oaks, CA: Sage.

Krebs, D. (1987). The challenge of altruism in biology and psychology. In C. Crawford, M. Smith, & D. Krebs (Eds.), *Sociobiology and psychology.* Hillsdale, NJ: Lawrence Erlbaum.

Langhorst, P., Schultz, G., & Lambertz, M. (1984). Oscillating neuronal network of the common brainstem system. In K. Miyakawa, H. P. Koepchen, & C. Polosa (Eds.), *Mechanics of blood pressure waves* (pp. 257–275). Tokyo: Japan Scientific Societies Press.

Lauriola, M., & Iani, L. (2015). Does positivity mediate the relation of extraversion and neuroticism with subjective happiness? *PloS One, 10*(3), e0121991. https://doi.org/10.1371/journal.pone.0121991

Lewicki, R. J., Wierthoff, C., & Tomlinson, E. C. (2005). What is the role of trust in organizational justice? In J. Greenberg &

J. A. Colquitt (Eds.), *Handbook of organizational justice* (pp. 247–270). Mahwah, NJ: Lawrence Erlbaum.

Lewis, M. (2009, February 13). The no-stats all-star. *New York Times Magazine.* www.nytimes.com/2009/02/15/magazine/15Battier-t.html

Lieberson, S., & O'Connor, J. (1972). Leadership and organizational performance: A study of large corporations. *American Sociological Review, 37*(2), 117–130.

Loeb, J., & Northrop, J. H. (1917). Heliotropic animals as photometers on the basis of the validity of the Bunsen-Roscoe Law for heliotropic reactions. *National Academy of Sciences, 3*(9), 539–544.

Lunenburg, F. C. (2012). Power and leadership: An influence process. *International Journal of Management, Business, and Administration, 15,* 1–9.

MacIntyre, A. (1984). *After virtue: A study in moral theory* (2nd ed.). Notre Dame, IN: University of Notre Dame Press.

Małgorzata Szcześniak, M., Colaço, M., & Rondón, G. (2012). Development of interpersonal trust among children and adolescents. *Polish Psychological Bulletin, 43,* 50–58.

Malhotra, D., & Lumineau, F. (2011). Trust and collaboration in the aftermath of conflict. *Academy of Management Journal, 54,* 981–998.

Martinek, K., & Berezin, I. V. (1979). Artificial light-sensitive enzymatic systems as chemical amplifiers of weak light signals. *Photochemistry and Photobiology, 29,* 637–650.

Maslow, A. H. (1968). *Toward a psychology of being.* New York, NY: Van Nostrand.

McCraty, R. (2002). Influence of cardiac afferent input on heart-brain synchronization and cognitive performance. *International Journal of Psychophysiology, 45,* 72–73.

McCraty, R. (2016). Exploring the role of the heart in human performance: An overview of the research conducted by the HeartMath Institute. In *Science of the Heart* (Vol. 2, pp. 53–66). Boulder Creek, CA: HeartMath Institute.

McCraty, R., & Childre, D. (2004). The grateful heart: The psychophysiology of appreciation. In R. A. Emmons and M. E.

McCullough (Eds.), *The psychology of gratitude* (pp. 230–255). New York, NY: Oxford University Press.

McGregor, D. (1960). *The human side of enterprise.* New York, NY: McGraw-Hill.

Merton, R. K. (1968). *Social organization and social structure.* New York, NY: Free Press.

Meyer, M. (2018). The evolution and challenges of the concept of organizational virtuousness in positive organizational scholarship. *Journal of Business Ethics, 153,* 245–264.

Miller, G. F. (2007). Sexual selection for moral virtues. *The Quarterly Review of Biology, 82,* 97–125.

Mishra, A. K., & Mishra, K. E. (2013). *Becoming a trustworthy leader.* New York, NY: Routledge.

Mishra, A. K., & Spreitzer, G. M. (1998). Explaining how survivors respond to downsizing: The roles of trust, empowerment, justice, and work design. *Academy of Management Review, 23,* 567–588.

Morholt, E., Bradwein, P. F., & Joseph, A. (1966). *A sourcebook for the biological sciences.* New York, NY: Harcourt, Brace, and World, Inc.

Mrosovsky, N., & Kingsmill, S. F. (1985). How turtles find the sea. *Zeitschrift Fur Tierpsychologie-Journal of Comparative Ethology, 67,* 237–256.

Nightingale, F. (1860). *Notes on nursing: What it is and what it is not* (2nd ed.). London, England: Harrison.

Northrop, J. H., & Loeb, J. (1923). The photochemical basis of animal heliotropism. *Journal of General Physiology, 5,* 581–595.

Okun, M. A., Yeung, E. W., & Brown, S. (2013). Volunteering by older adults and risk of mortality: A meta-analysis. *Psychology and Aging, 28*(2), 564–577.

Ou, A. Y., Tsui, A. S., Kinicki, A., Waldman, D., Song, L. J., & Xiao, Z. X. (2014). Understanding humble chief executive officers: Connections to top management team integration and middle manager responses. *Administrative Science Quarterly, 59,* 34–72.

Owens, B., Baker, W., Sumpter, D., & Cameron, K. (2016). Relational energy at work: Implications for job engagement and job performance. *Journal of Applied Psychology, 101,* 35–49.

Owens, B., & Hekman, D. (2012). Modeling how to grow: An inductive examination of humble leader behaviors, contingencies, and outcomes. *Academy of Management Journal, 55,* 787–818.

Owens, B., Johnson, M., & Mitchell, T. (2013). Expressed humility in organizations: Implications for performance, teams, and leadership. *Organization Science, 24,* 1517–1538.

Owens, B. P., Rowatt, W. C., & Wilkins, A. L. (2012). Exploring the relevance and implications of humility in organizations. In K. S. Cameron & G. M. Spreitzer (Eds.), *The Oxford handbook of positive organizational scholarship* (pp. 260–272). New York, NY: Oxford University Press.

Owens, B. P., Sumpter, D. M., Cameron, K. S., & Baker, W. E. (2018, May 28). *Relational energy and well-being.* Presented at the Cesar Ritz Well-being Conference, Brigg, Switzerland.

Peterson, C., Park, N., Hall, N., & Seligman, M. E. P. (2009). Zest at work. *Journal of Organizational Behavior, 30,* 161–172.

Peterson, C., & Seligman, M. E. P. (2004). *Character strengths and virtues.* New York, NY: Oxford University Press.

Pink, D. H. (2009). *Drive: The surprising truth about what motivates us.* New York, NY: Riverhead Books.

Pinker, S. (1997). *How the mind works.* New York, NY: W.W. Norton.

Pressman, S. D., & Cohen, S. (2005). Does positive affect influence health? *Psychological Bulletin, 131,* 925–971.

Pressman, S. D., & Cohen, S. (2012). Positive emotion words and longevity in famous deceased psychologists. *Health Psychology, 31,* 297–305.

Pressman, S. D., Jenkins, B., & Moskowitz, J. (2019). Positive affect and health: What do we know and where next should we go? *Annual Review of Psychology, 70,* 627–650.

Quinn, R. E. (2015). *The positive organization.* San Francisco, CA: Berrett-Koehler.

Quinn, R. W., Spreitzer, G. M., & Lam, C. F. (2012). Building a sustainable model of human energy in organizations: Exploring the critical role of resources. *Academy of Management Annals, 6,* 1–60.

Redwine, L. S., Henry, B. L., Pung, M. A., Wilson, K., Chinh, K., Knight, B., . . . Mills, P. J. (2018). Pilot randomized study of a gratitude journaling intervention on heart rate variability and inflammatory biomarkers in patients with Stage B heart failure. *Psychosomatic Medicine, 78,* 667–676. doi:10.1097/PSY.0000000000000316

Romanes, C. J. (1893). Experiments in heliotropism. *Proceedings of the Royal Society of London, 54,* 333–335.

Roth-Hanania, R., Davidov, M., & Zahn-Waxler, C. (2011). Empathy development from 8 to 16 months: Early signs of concern for others. *Infant Behavior and Development, 34,* 447–458.

Rothschild, N. (2020, March 24). Sweden is open for business during its coronavirus outbreak: The Scandinavian country believes its distinctive high-trust culture will protect it from needing to shut down for the pandemic. *Foreign Policy.* https://foreignpolicy.com/2020/03/24/sweden-coronavirus-open-for-business

Rowe, R., & Calnan, M. (2006). Trust relations in health care: Developing a theoretical framework from the new NHS. *Journal of Health Organization and Management, 20,* 376–396.

Russek, L. G., & Schwartz, G. E. (1997). Feelings of parental caring predict health status in midlife: A 35-year follow-up of the Harvard Mastery of Stress study. *Journal of Behavioral Medicine, 20,* 1–13.

Ryan, R. M., & Deci, E. L. (2017). *Self-determination theory.* New York, NY: Guilford Press.

Ryff, C. D., & Singer, B. (Eds.). (2001). *Emotion, social relationships, and health.* Oxford, England: Oxford University Press.

Schwartz, C., & Sender, R. (1991). Helping others helps oneself: Response shift effects to peer support. *Social Science and Medicine, 48,* 1563–1575.

Seppala, E. C. (2017). *The happiness track: How to apply the science of happiness to accelerate your success.* New York, NY: Harper Collins.

Seppala, E. C., Simon-Thomas, E., Brown, S. L., Worline, M. C., Cameron, D., & Doty, J. R. (2017). *The Oxford handbook of compassion science.* New York, NY: Oxford University Press.

Sharot, T., Riccardi, A. M., Raio, C. M., & Phelps, E. A. (2007). Neural mechanisms mediating optimism bias. *Nature, 450,* 102–106.

Sison, A. G. (2008). *Corporate governance and ethics: An Aristotelian perspective.* Northampton, MA: Edward Elgar Publishing.

Sloane, S., Baillargeon, R., & Premack, D. (2012). Do infants have a sense of fairness? *Psychological Science, 23,* 196–204.

Smillie, L. D., DeYoung, C. G., & Hall, P. J. (2015). Clarifying the relation between extraversion and positive affect. *Personality, 83,* 564–574.

Smith, J. (2019, November 20). Is positive psychology all it's cracked up to be? *Vox.* https://www.vox.com/the-highlight /2019/11/13/20955328/

Smith, J. C., & Baker, H. D. (1960). Conditioning in the horseshoe crab. *Journal of Comparative and Physiological Psychology, 53,* 279–281.

Snyder, C. R., & Lopez, S. J. (2002). *Handbook of positive psychology.* New York, NY: Oxford University Press.

Spreitzer, G., Bacevice, P., Hendricks, H., & Garrett, P. (2021). Thriving in the new world of work: Implications for organizational community. In *Research in Organizational Change and Development, 6,* 1–60. New York: Emerald Insight.

Stroebe, M., Stroebe, W., & Hansson, R. (1988). Bereavement research: An historical introduction. *Journal of Social Issues, 44,* 1–18.

Surian, L., & Franchin, L. (2017). Toddlers selectively help fair agents. *Frontiers in Psychology, 8,* 944. doi:10.3389/fpsyg.2017 .00944

Szulanski, G., Cappette, R., & Jensen, R. J. (2004). When and how trustworthiness matters. *Organizational Science, 15,* 600–613.

Tangney, P., Stuewig, J., & Mashek, D. (2007). Moral emotions and moral behavior. *Annual Review of Psychology, 58,* 345–372.

Tenny, E. R., Poole, J. M., & Diener, E. (2016). Does positivity enhance work performance? Why, when, and what we don't know. *Research in Organizational Behavior, 36,* 27–46.

Thomas, A. (1988). Does leadership make a difference to organizational performance? *Administrative Science Quarterly, 33*(3), 388–400.

Thomas, K. W. (2009). *Intrinsic motivation at work: Building energy and commitment* (2nd ed.). San Francisco, CA: Berrett-Koehler.

Thompson, C. (2019, September). Out of the shadows: The impacts of light on human health. *Lighting Newswire, 233,* 69–77.

Tiller, W. A., McCraty, R., & Atkinson, M. (1996). Cardiac coherence: A new, noninvasive measure of autonomic nervous system order. *Alternative Therapies on Health and Medicine, 2,* 56–65.

Van de Vondervoort, J., & Hamlin, J. K. (2018). The early emergence of sociomoral evaluation: Infants prefer prosocial others. *Current Opinion in Psychology, 20,* 77–81.

Vanette, D., & Cameron, K. S. (2015). *Implementing positive organizational scholarship at Prudential.* Center for Positive Organizations, Ann Arbor, University of Michigan.

Van Nuys, D. (2010, November 3). Popping the happiness bubble: The backlash against positive psychology. *Psychology Today.* https://www.psychologytoday.com/us/blog/the-happiness -dispatch/201011/popping-the-happiness-bubble-the-backlash -against-positive

Vera, D., & Rodriguez-Lopez, A. (2004). Humility as a source of competitive advantage. *Organizational Dynamics, 33,* 393–408.

Walch, J. M., Rabin, B. A., Day, R., Williams, J. N., Choi, K., Kang, J. D. (2005). The effect of sunlight on postoperative analgesic medication use: A prospective study of patients undergoing surgery. *Psychosomatic Medicine, 67,* 157–163.

Wang, C. S., Galinsky, A. D., & Murnigham, J. K. (2009). Bad drives psychological reactions, but good propels behavior. *Psychological Science, 20,* 634–644.

Warneken, F., & Tomasello, M. (2006). Altruistic helping in human infants and young chimpanzees. *Science, 311,* 1301–1303.

Weick, K. (1984). Small wins: Redefining the scale of social problems. *American Psychologist, 39:* 4049.

Weiner, N. O. (1993). *The harmony of the soul: Mental health and moral virtue reconsidered.* Albany: State University of New York Press.

Willans, A., Dunn, W., Sandstrom, G., & Madden, K. (2016). Is spending money on others good for your heart? *Health Psychology, 35*(6), 574–583. doi:10.1037/hea0000332

Williams, D. A. (2016). Cognitive-behavioral therapy in central sensitivity syndromes. *Current Rheumatology Review, 12,* 2–12.

Wong, P. T. P., & Roy, S. (2018). Critique of positive psychology and positive interventions. In N. J. L. Brown, T. Lomas, & F. J. Eiroa-Orosa (Eds.), *The Routledge international handbook of critical positive psychology* (pp. 142–160). London: Routledge/Taylor & Francis Group.

Wong, Y. J., Owen, J., Gabana, N. T., Brown, J. W., McInnis, S., Toth, P., & Gilman, L. (2018). Does gratitude writing improve the mental health of psychotherapy clients? Evidence from a randomized controlled trial. *Psychotherapy Research, 28,* 192–202. doi:10.1080/10503307.2016.1169332

Worline, M. C., Dutton, J. E., & Hardin, A. E. (2015, October 6). Forming stronger bonds with people at work. *Harvard Business Review.* https://hbr.org/2017/10/forming-stronger-bonds-with-people-at-work

Xia, Y., Gupta, G. K., Castano, A. P., Mroz, P., Avci, P., and Hamblin, M. R. (2014). CpG oligodeoxynucleotide as immune adjuvant enhances photodynamic therapy response in murine metastatic breast cancer. *Journal of Biophotonics, 7*(11–12), 897–905.

Yancey, D., Greger, H., & Coburn, P. (1990). Determinants of grief resolution in cancer death. *Journal of Palliative Care, 6,* 24–31.

Yang, Y., & Konrad, A. M. (2011). Diversity and organizational innovation: The role of employee involvement. *Journal of Organizational Behavior, 32,* 1062–1083.

Zak, P. J. (2017, January–February). The neuroscience of trust. *Harvard Business Review,* pp. 84–90.

# INDEX

☀ ABOUT THE AUTHOR

Kim Cameron became interested in positively energizing leadership as a result of studying organizational downsizing in the United States during the 1980s and 1990s. In those research projects, he discovered that a majority of organizations that abolished jobs, eliminated employees, consolidated activities, and retrenched operations also experienced a number of negative, dysfunctional outcomes he referred to as the dirty dozen.

A key finding from those research projects was not surprising: almost all organizations deteriorate in performance after downsizing. On the other hand, he observed a few organizations that thrived. Despite the fact that financial losses were severe, employees were involuntarily terminated, the organization experienced contraction and consolidation, the future was uncertain, and senior executives made unpleasant decisions, these organizations flourished. He reached the conclusion that organizations that flourish after a downsizing experience are characterized by virtuousness—institutionalized compassion, forgiveness, gratitude, trustworthiness, optimism, and integrity, to name just a few attributes.

That discovery led him to a 20-year investigation of the impact of virtuousness on organizations and their employees. He discovered that when leaders demonstrate virtuousness, they produce *positive energy*, which, in turn, has a major impact on performance. The empirically validated prescriptions as well as the practical implications of this research led to his being recognized as among the top 10 scholars in the organizational sciences whose work has been most frequently downloaded from Google. This book summarizes some of the important outcomes of that research.

He is the William Russell Kelly Professor of Management and Organizations in the Ross School of Business and professor of higher education in the School of Education at the University of Michigan. He is a cofounder of the discipline of positive organizational scholarship—the scientific study of what produces extraordinary performance in organizations and their employees. His research on organizational virtuousness and the development of cultures of abundance has been published in more than 140 academic articles and 15 scholarly books.

He has served as dean of the Weatherhead School of Management at Case Western Reserve University, associate dean in the Marriott School of Business at Brigham Young University, and as associate dean and academic department chair in the Ross School of Business at the University of Michigan. He actively consults with business organizations on five continents, federal and military organizations, and health-care and educational organizations. He received BS and MS degrees from Brigham Young University and MA and PhD degrees from Yale University. He is married to the former Melinda Cummings and has seven children.

Also by Kim Cameron

Positive Organizational Scholarship
Foundations of a New Discipline
**Edited by Kim S. Cameron, Jane E. Dutton,
and Robert E. Quinn**

Just as positive psychology focuses on exploring optimal individual
psychological states rather than pathological ones, *Positive Organizational Scholarship* focuses attention on optimal organizational
states—the dynamics in organizations that lead to the development
of human strength; foster resiliency in employees; make healing,
restoration, and reconciliation possible; and cultivate extraordinary
individual and organizational performance. Written by internationally renowned scholars and authors, this book offers practical guid-
ance for managers and a future research agenda for understanding
and enabling positive organizational behavior.

Hardcover, ISBN 978-1-57675-232-6
PDF ebook, ISBN 978-1-57675-966-0
ePub ebook, ISBN 978-1-60509-438-0

Berrett–Koehler Publishers, Inc.
www.bkconnection.com   **800.929.2929**

Also by Kim Cameron
Positive Leadership
Strategies for Extraordinary Performance, Second Ed.

In this concise, inspiring, and practical guide, Cameron describes four positive leadership strategies, lays out a proven process for implementing them, and includes a self-assessment instrument. This second edition has been updated throughout with new research findings and new ideas for implementing positive leadership.

Paperback, ISBN 978-1-60994-566-4
PDF ebook, ISBN 978-1-60994-567-1
ePub ebook, ISBN 978-1-60994-568-8
Digital audio, ISBN 978-1-5230-8814-0

Practicing Positive Leadership
Tools and Techniques That Create Extraordinary Results

Plenty of research has been done on why companies go terribly wrong, but what makes companies go spectacularly right? That's the question that Kim Cameron asked over a decade ago. Since then, Cameron and his colleagues have uncovered the principles and practices that set extraordinarily effective organizations apart from the merely successful.

Paperback, ISBN 978-1-60994-972-3
PDF ebook, ISBN 978-1-60994-973-0
ePub ebook, ISBN 978-1-60994-974-7

Berrett–Koehler Publishers, Inc.
www.bkconnection.com   **800.929.2929**

Dear reader,

Thank you for picking up this book and welcome to the worldwide BK community! You're joining a special group of people who have come together to create positive change in their lives, organizations, and communities.

What's BK all about?

Our mission is to connect people and ideas to create a world that works for all.

Why? Our communities, organizations, and lives get bogged down by old paradigms of self-interest, exclusion, hierarchy, and privilege. But we believe that can change. That's why we seek the leading experts on these challenges—and share their actionable ideas with you.

A welcome gift

To help you get started, we'd like to offer you a **free copy** of one of our bestselling ebooks:

www.bkconnection.com/welcome

When you claim your **free ebook**, you'll also be subscribed to our blog.

Our freshest insights

Access the best new tools and ideas for leaders at all levels on our blog at ideas.bkconnection.com.

Sincerely,

Your friends at Berrett-Koehler